LOMELINO'S PIES

LOMELINO'S PIES LINDA LOMELINO

A SWEET CELEBRATION OF PIES, GALETTES & TARTS

BOULDER | 2017

| CONTENTS |

| PREFACE |

If I were forced to choose one type of baked good to make for the rest of my life, it would be pies. For me, there is something almost magical about baking pies. Everything from pinching the butter into the flour to preparing wonderfully spicy apple filling or seeing the pie dough become so beautifully golden in the oven. It is all pure magic for me—that something so easy can be so fantastic with just a few ingredients.

It is easy to think that there is only one way to bake a pie, but that isn't so. Far from it. There are so many types of pies—pies with decorated crusts in all different forms, crumble pies, minipies, pies on a stick, fried pies. . . . Yes, the list can get long. In addition, there is a rich variety of fruits and berries to bake into a fine crust that, in turn, can be varied in ever so many ways. And we all have our favorite flavors and types.

No matter whether you choose to bake a chocolate pie with peanut butter or a galette with strawberries and rhubarb, I can promise that you will not be disappointed. With a dollop of whipped cream on top, a scoop of homemade vanilla ice cream, or a spoonful of vanilla cream, it will be exceedingly good.
/Linda

| PIE SCHOOL |

Single-crust pies, pies with a crumble topping, or double-crust pies: here are a few things to consider so your pies will be as good as possible.

Ingredients

FLOUR. I use regular all-purpose flour for piecrust dough, sometimes in combination with nut flour. Pie dough with nut flour will be a bit more fragile but unbelievably fine and crisp. I buy prepared almond flour, but I also like making my own nut flour, which should be ground from toasted nuts, as follows:

Preheat the oven to 350°F and toast the nuts on a baking sheet or in an ovenproof pan for 6 to 10 minutes, depending on the type of nuts. Make sure that the nuts don't burn, which can happen quickly at the end of the baking time. Cool the nuts completely and then grind them to a fine flour in a blender or food processor. Sometimes it can be difficult to grind the nuts very finely, in which case it helps to mix in a little all-purpose flour (from the ingredients for the pie dough) with the nuts and then pulse them again.

You might also try substituting various kinds of wholegrain flour for part of the all-purpose flour, such as rye flour or graham flour. However, don't use too much of the wholegrain flour, as it can result in a dry pie shell.

Sometimes I add spices to the pastry, such as a little ground cardamom or cinnamon, or something similar.

BUTTER. I always use regular salted butter with 80 percent fat content unless otherwise specified.

If the instructions in the recipe do not indicate anything else, the butter should always be well chilled so that the piecrust will get good and flaky when it is baked. For the best results, measure the amount of butter you need, dice it, and freeze it for 5 to 10 minutes before using.

SUGAR. As a rule of thumb, I use four types of sugar: regular white granulated sugar, light Muscovado sugar, Turbinado sugar, and confectioners' sugar.

I use granulated sugar most often for pie dough and fillings.

Light Muscovado sugar can be good in fillings. It adds a subtle caramel flavor. If you cannot source Muscovado, brown sugar works well too.

I also use Turbinado sugar in certain fillings, but most of all, I sprinkle it on top of the pie before baking it—it adds a crispy layer. If you don't have Turbinado sugar at home to sprinkle on top of the pie, you can use raw cane sugar or granulated sugar instead.

I use confectioners' (powdered) sugar primarily for sifting on top of pies after they have been baked and immediately before serving, primarily for its appearance. This can also be a good trick to use when you don't think the pie is sweet enough.

SALT. When salt is included in the ingredients list, it means sea salt. Crush the flakes with your fingers or lightly grind them in a mortar and then measure the salt with a measuring spoon. If you don't have any sea salt on hand, use regular pouring salt, but decrease the amount by half.

LIQUID FOR THE DOUGH. In order for the dough to be flaky, the water added to it should be very cold.

Fill a glass with cold water, add a few ice cubes, and let it stand for a few minutes.

When adding water to the pie dough, add only a tablespoon of water at a time. There should be only just enough water to hold the dough together.

Sometimes I substitute buttermilk, sour milk, or crème fraîche for a part (or all) of the water for pie dough. To add a little extra flavor, you can also use Cointreau, cognac, vodka, dark rum, or beer.

Making Pie Dough

Mix the flour, salt, and sugar in a bowl and add the diced, cold butter. Pinch the butter with your fingers or use a knife to mix it with the dry ingredients. You do not need to be overly meticulous. It is better to have small bits of butter remaining in the dough. I personally like to use my hands because I think it is the easiest way to control the results. Even a food processor will work, but be careful, as you do not want to overwork the dough.

After the butter has been worked in, add the water, one tablespoon at a time. Mix it with a fork to distribute the liquid evenly. There is enough water when you can pick up a bit of the dough and it coheres when you press it together. The dough absolutely should not be kneaded because then the gluten in the pie dough will start to develop and you won't get that crisp and flaky result you are after. You want the dough to just come together. Cover the dough with a piece of plastic wrap, flatten out the dough slightly, and then completely wrap the dough with plastic wrap and refrigerate it for at least 1 hour, but preferably overnight.

Preparing the pie dough the evening before saves a lot of time when the pie needs to be baked. Maybe it sounds like a long process, but as soon as you have the hang of it, you can easily make a pie dough in just a few minutes.

Rolling Out Pie Dough

If the pie dough feels too cold and hard to roll out, let it stand at room temperature (in the plastic wrap so it won't dry out) for 5 to 20 minutes before rolling it out.

Make sure that the work surface is floured, and rotate the dough as you roll it out. That is to say, roll, lift the dough and turn it, sprinkle more flour on the work surface, and continue rolling as necessary. As soon as you begin rolling out the dough, the small bits of butter will melt from the heat. If you feel that the dough is getting too warm, you can put it in the freezer for a few minutes so it will quickly get cold again.

If you have a problem with the dough sticking, you can roll it out between two pieces of parchment paper. That also makes it easier to transfer the dough to the pie pan.

Make sure you roll out the dough enough so it will fill the pan when baked. It should be larger than the diameter of your pie pan because you have to include the height at each side plus some overhang. For a 6-inch-diameter pan, the dough should be rolled out to about 9 inches, depending on how high you want the edge. If you want to calculate precisely how much to roll out the dough, use a measuring tape to measure the bottom of the pan plus the height of the sides.

After the dough has been rolled out, it will be easiest to transfer it to the pie pan by first carefully rolling it up onto the rolling pin and then laying it over the pie pan. Cover the pan with the pie dough and trim off any excess dough, leaving an overhang of ¾ to 1½ inches. You will need the overhang for securing the top crust or, for open-top pies, because the shell can shrink slightly when baking.

When this is all done, place the pie pan in the refrigerator while you roll out the top crust. If you keep the crust cold, the pie dough will hold its shape better and shrink less as it bakes.

Crumble Dough

A crumble is the simplest form of pie dough. It doesn't need to be rolled out and will thus be more porous in character. It doesn't matter much if the butter is cold or room temperature. Crumble dough is also fun to vary with different kinds of grains, nuts, and seeds or—why not?—various spices, such as cinnamon, cardamom, or grated ginger. Select or reject from your favorite nuts and spices.

Flaky Pastry Dough

Making their own flaky pastry dough is definitely something that scares people. A traditional flaky pastry dough recipe takes a long time to work, easily half a day. I wanted to find a simpler way to make flaky pastry, and so I created this recipe. For this version, you don't need to roll in the butter between turns as for traditional pastry dough, but the dough still puffs up quite well and will be tender and crisp.

Easy Flaky Pastry Dough

¾ cup all-purpose flour
9 tablespoons (4½ ounces) cold butter
4–5 tablespoons ice-cold water

1. Pour the flour into a stainless steel bowl. Dice the butter and add it to the flour. Put the mixture in the freezer for 10 minutes.
2. Pinch the butter and flour together. If the butter becomes too warm, refrigerate the flour mixture for a few minutes.
3. Make a well in the middle of the mixture and add the ice-cold water, a tablespoon at a time, stirring in the water with a fork as you pour. The dough should only just cohere but not feel dry. If you pick up a bit of dough and it holds together when you pinch it, the dough has enough water.
4. Turn the dough out onto a lightly floured work surface, press it into a rectangle, and then roll out the dough to approximately 4¾ x 11 inches. Brush off any excess flour and fold the long edges over by one-third, overlapping the edges, making three layers (in baker's language). Next, turn the dough a quarter turn and roll it once again to 4¾ x 11 inches. Brush off any excess flour and fold in the edges as above. Repeat this process 4 more times so that you've rolled and folded a total of 6 times. If the dough starts to feel warm between each step, cover it with plastic wrap and put it in the freezer for a few minutes.
5. Cover the dough with plastic wrap and let it rest in the refrigerator for 1 hour, preferably overnight.

Lattice-Top Crust

A lattice is the most classic pattern for a top crust, and it works in any situation when you want a pie with a crust. Believe it or not, a basket weave pattern made with woven strips of dough is actually not as difficult to make as it looks.

You can decide if you want to cut wide or narrow strips. Narrow strips require much more work than wider strips.

It is important that the pie filling has cooled completely before you pour it into the pie pan and weave the crust; otherwise, the dough strips will soften and make the job so much harder.

Begin by cutting the number of strips that you need. It doesn't matter if a few are shorter, because you can always use them for the edges. For this pie, I cut eight strips, four for each direction.

1. Place four strips vertically.

2. Fold strip numbers 1 and 3 back to the middle of the pie.

3. Place a horizontal strip immediately above the center. Unfold strips 1 and 3 over it.

4. Fold strips 2 and 4 back over the horizontal strip.

5. Place a horizontal strip at the top of the pie. Unfold strips 2 and 4 over it.

6. Fold strips 2 and 4 back from the bottom of the pie toward the center and place a horizontal strip immediately below the center.

7. Unfold strips 2 and 4 over the horizontal strip.

8. Fold strips 1 and 3 back from the bottom of the pie toward the center.

9. Lay a horizontal strip at the bottom of the pie.

10. Fold down strips 1 and 3. Attach all of the ends to the bottom crust with a little water (which you can brush all around the edge) and fold them down. Ends should be trimmed and the edges crimped.

Other Types of Top Crusts and Decorations

SOLID CRUST. Simply roll out the pie dough for the top crust so that it will cover the filling. Roll the dough out somewhat larger than the top diameter of the pie pan. Brush the edges of the pie shell with water and place the top crust over the filling. Press the dough together along the edge and, if you like, make a pattern, or cut away some of the overhanging dough and use the tines of a fork to make a pattern.

After you have brushed the pie with an egg wash, finish by cutting a couple of slits in the crust so the steam can escape.

HOLES. A solid top crust full of holes will look nice, and you won't need to cut any slits in the dough for the steam to escape. Use a piping tip or a thimble to punch out the holes, or use small cookie cutters of various shapes, such as stars or hearts. Follow the directions for the solid crust (above) for attaching the crust on top of the pie.

DOTS AND LEAVES. Decorate the piecrust or edges with the leftover pie dough. Punch out patterns with a piping tip or a cookie cutter. Cut leaves with a small knife.

BRAIDS. You can try braids to decorate the edge around a pie or to substitute for regular strips in a lattice pattern. It takes a little work, but it will look so pretty.

Cut out a long strip of pie dough to the width you prefer. Cut the strip into 3 narrower strips, leaving the piece intact across at the top (imagine a pair of pants with three legs). Braid the dough and attach it to the edge of the pie with a little water.

ROPE. Dough twisted into a rope looks great around the pie edge, but it requires more dough than other decorations. Roll out two equal pieces of dough and twist them together. Attach the rope around the edge of the pie with some water.

CRIMPED EDGE. Without a doubt, the crimped-edge technique is one I use most often for my pies because it is so effective and so unbelievably easy to make.

Trim the dough slightly larger than the pie and fold the dough over to the outside. Use your fingers to pinch the edge into a zigzag shape.

If you use a solid top crust, you should first attach it to the bottom crust with a little water, then cut off or even

out the edge of the top crust for a narrow overhang, leaving about an inch of dough all around. Now fold the edge all around, either under the pie along the edge of the pie pan or up toward the top of the pie, and then crimp the edge.

If the Dough Splits

If your dough splits, it's not the end of the world. Just take a bit of dough and cover the splits or holes by pressing and smoothing out the patch with your fingers. It won't affect the finished results.

If you get a hole or split in the top crust, you can always cut out a pattern, such as a heart or a leaf, with leftover dough and cover the "wound" with that.

Leftover Dough

In many of the recipes in this book, there will be a little pie dough left over, because it is better to have too much dough than too little. Leftover dough is perfect for freezing to use later. You can roll out the extra dough and cut out a design that might, for example, be pretty for garnishing a crumble pie. Just keep in mind that pie dough can't be rolled out over and over again. After the third time, it is likely to become tough and simply won't be as good.

Saving Pie Dough

You can prepare pie dough up to two days ahead of time if you keep it cold. Make sure that you wrap it completely in plastic wrap so that it won't absorb the smells of anything else in the refrigerator.

Pie dough freezes exceptionally well, sometimes for several months. To freeze dough, make sure it is completely covered with plastic wrap and then put it in a tightly sealed plastic freezer bag. Flatten out the dough before you freeze it so that it will thaw more quickly. Mark the bag with the date so you won't forget when you made it.

To thaw the dough, transfer it from the freezer to the refrigerator and leave it in overnight before you use it. The dough can also be thawed at room temperature, but that might make it a little too moist.

Freezing a Whole Pie

You can also freeze a whole, fruit-filled pie or galette unbaked. If you do this, wait until you're ready to bake it to brush on the egg wash.

You do not need to thaw the pie before baking, just apply the egg wash, cut a few air holes, sprinkle the dough with sugar, and put it in the oven. The pie might need a longer baking time—up to 10 to 15 minutes longer—if it goes directly from the freezer to the oven.

Consider using a pie pan that will tolerate quick temperature changes—it should be able to go from the freezer to an oven heated as high as 435°F. Glass or porcelain is not a good choice in this situation (it is risky even if the pan is ovenproof). Instead, I recommend a metal pie pan or even a single-use pie pan (which is perfect if you want to prepare the pie well ahead of time or you need to bake several pies).

Cream-filled pies, such as Coconut Cream Pie (page 116), or pies topped with meringue should not be frozen.

Choosing a Pie Pan

I think metal pie pans are the best because they distribute the heat well, which, in turn, makes the pie shell nice and crisp. Sometimes I use glass or porcelain pans, but primarily for crumble pies that do not have a shell. Do not bake crumble pies in a springform pan with a removable bottom. They are not always completely tight, and the pie can leak out into the oven—believe me, I've tried. . . .

The diameter given in the recipes corresponds to the bottom of the pan.

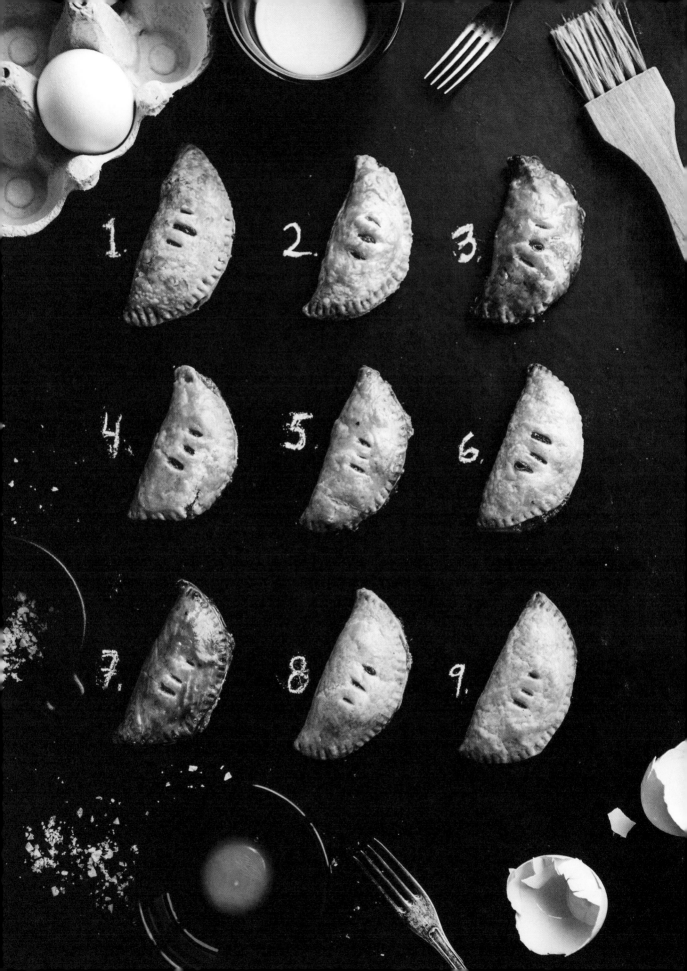

Pie Fillings

APPLE AND PEAR. I like to use firm, rather tart apples to make pies. Ingrid Marie and Aroma are two Swedish types that I especially like to use for baking. Cortlands and Golden Delicious work beautifully as well. Apples that are too sweet or mealy in consistency will become mushy as they bake and, therefore, cannot be recommended for the best results.

When choosing pears for pie, they should also be relatively firm and not overly ripe, as they can easily get mushy. In general, overripe fruit is not ideal for baking pies.

CITRUS FRUIT. When choosing citrus fruit for pies, the choice of fruit is very important. I prefer using organic ingredients when I bake, particularly when it comes to citrus fruits, because most often it is just the zest that is used.

FROZEN COMPARED WITH FRESH BERRIES. Using frozen berries is excellent for crumble-top pies and galettes—even for pies with a top crust. But in that case I use precooked filling (see below) because otherwise it would be too moist.

For pies topped with berries, I recommend using fresh berries (see Easy Tart with Fresh Berries, page 97).

PRECOOKED PIE FILLING. In many cases, I choose to precook all the filling to prevent the release of too much liquid in the crust. This applies primarily to pies with fruit that exude a lot of liquid, such as cherries, strawberries, and apples. Even frozen berries and frozen fruit can release a lot of liquid. Precooking is used mostly for pies with a shell and some type of top crust, not for crumble pies.

The primary purpose of precooking filling is to prevent the bottom crust from becoming soggy and doughy as the pie bakes. Even when it comes to flavor concentration, I think that in many cases precooking the filling is better. As long as you have chosen fruit that is not overripe, the pieces of fruit will be soft but will still have structure and a little chew resistance.

The filling always shrinks during baking, something that can lead to a large space being created between the filling and the top crust (another reason to precook the filling). So that the fruit filling in a pie will have some stability and not just be a pool at the bottom of the pie shell, it needs some form of starch to bind the liquid and prepared filling. Most often I use flour or cornstarch because I almost always have them on hand, but tapioca or potato flour will also work. Another way to absorb the liquid is to mix 2 teaspoons of all-purpose flour with 2 teaspoons of granulated sugar and then sprinkle the bottom of the unbaked piecrust before adding the filling (see Classic Apple Pie, page 30).

LET THE FILLING COOL. The filling should never be warm when you pour it into the pie shell, no matter whether the shell is blind-baked or not. If you pour a warm filling into an unbaked pie shell, the butter in the dough will begin to melt. If you pour a warm filling into a blind-baked pie shell, the shell will soak up the moisture of the filling and soften.

Glazing the Pie

You can glaze a pie with various mixtures for different results. Almost always, I use an egg wash—an egg whisked with a pinch of salt and a tablespoon of milk.

If you want a completely egg-free pie, you can brush it with a splash of milk or cream instead.

If you want a milk-free pie, you can whisk the egg with a tablespoon of water instead.

You can also use a leftover egg white or egg yolk from a recipe to brush over the pie.

Of course, you could totally skip glazing the pie, but in that case, the pie will not have a beautiful golden-brown, shiny surface, and if you want to sprinkle sugar on it, it won't stick. The flavor will be good in any case, no matter what choices you make—it is entirely up to you.

In the photo to the left, you can see the approximate results of different types of glazes, as follows:

1. Nothing at all brushed on. The surface is matte and does not have much color.
2. Egg white. The surface is somewhat shiny and has little color.
3. Egg yolk. The surface is very shiny and has too much color.
4. A whole egg plus a pinch of salt plus 1 tablespoon of water. The surface is somewhat shiny and has some color.
5. A whole egg plus a pinch of salt plus 1 tablespoon of milk. The surface is shiny and has too much color.
6. Whipping cream. The surface is rather matte and has too little color.
7. Egg yolk plus whipping cream. The surface is very shiny and there is much too much color.
8. Egg white plus water. The surface is matte and has too little color.
9. Milk. The surface is matte and has too little color.

Note that those crusts that are matte also hold their shape better, and you can see the stripes from the fork more clearly. If you have made a nice pattern with many details, it would be a good idea to glaze the pie with choices 6, 8, or 9, or choose 1 (no glaze at all).

Blind-Baking, or Prebaking, a Piecrust

Blind-baking a piecrust means that you bake only the pie shell in the pan, without any filling. Usually you should prick the shell with a fork and then lay parchment paper on the pie shell, fill the shell with uncooked rice or beans, and bake it until the pie dough is either half or completely baked. A blind-baked pie shell should always be cool before you pour in the filling.

You might blind-bake a pie shell for various reasons. For instance, if the filling for the pie shouldn't be cooked, the pie shell has to be blind-baked (for example, see Banana Cream Pie, page 114). Another reason can be that the filling contains so much liquid that the pie shell must be blind-baked so it doesn't become soggy.

As much as possible, I avoid prebaking pie dough that consists of flour, sugar, salt, butter, and water (in other words, the most common type of dough). Blind-baked pie shells have a tendency to shrink noticeably, and it is easier to attach an unbaked top crust to an unbaked bottom crust. The recipes in this book do not require a blind-baked pie shell unless otherwise stated.

Types of pie shells that I blind-bake include graham cracker shell (see S'mores Pie, page 120, and Banoffee Pie with Honeycomb, page 121), and shortcrust pastry (see Citrus Meringue Pie, page 110).

WHY IS A FILLED PIE COOLED IN THE FREEZER?

It is good to transfer a filled pie to the freezer 15 minutes before baking so that the pie can hold its shape and won't shrink as much in the oven. As the pie cools, the butter in the crust will chill again and won't melt as quickly when the pie is baked.

Baking a Pie

I usually bake pies at a high temperature to begin with and then reduce the heat. I do this primarily so the pie dough can firm up and bake quickly, thus holding its shape, and also so the pie will take on a good color.

One tip is to place a baking sheet in the oven as it preheats and then bake the pie on the baking sheet. This way you avoid spills in the oven. I also think the baking sheet functions the same way as a pizza stone—it heats the bottom of the pie and helps to bake the bottom crust more quickly. It is never good to have moist pie dough in the crust.

If you think that the edges of the pie are beginning to take on too much color, you can move the pie down to a lower rack in the oven and bake it there for the rest of the time, or you can cover the parts getting too dark with aluminum foil or parchment paper.

Let the Pie Cool

Let the pie cool completely (or almost) before you cut into it. The filling needs time to stabilize. If you cut the pie as soon as it is out of the oven, the filling will run out.

This doesn't apply to crumble pies, which are fine for eating while still warm (the berries still need to cool for a little while, though, to prevent burning your tongue).

Storing and Shelf Life

You can store a pie at room temperature for one day. For the longest shelf life, the pie should be covered with plastic wrap and refrigerated.

Different types of pies have different shelf lives. A pie with a very moist filling is really good for only a few days because the pie shell quickly absorbs the moisture and softens.

Pies topped with whipped cream should be eaten as quickly as possible. If you prepare the pie the day before, you should refrigerate it and add the whipped cream only immediately before serving (for example, Lime Pie with Coconut and White Chocolate, page 107).

One tip is to serve the whipped cream on the side so you can whip only as much as you need if you are serving just one or two pieces.

A baked fruit pie (such as Classic Apple Pie, page 30) can last up to five days in the refrigerator but is best the first two days. If you know that you are not going to eat the entire pie, you can cut it into pieces and freeze the pieces in a freezer container or something similar. That way, it will be easy to thaw only one piece of pie when you are tempted.

This is not the ideal way to eat it, but it's better than wasting delicious pie!

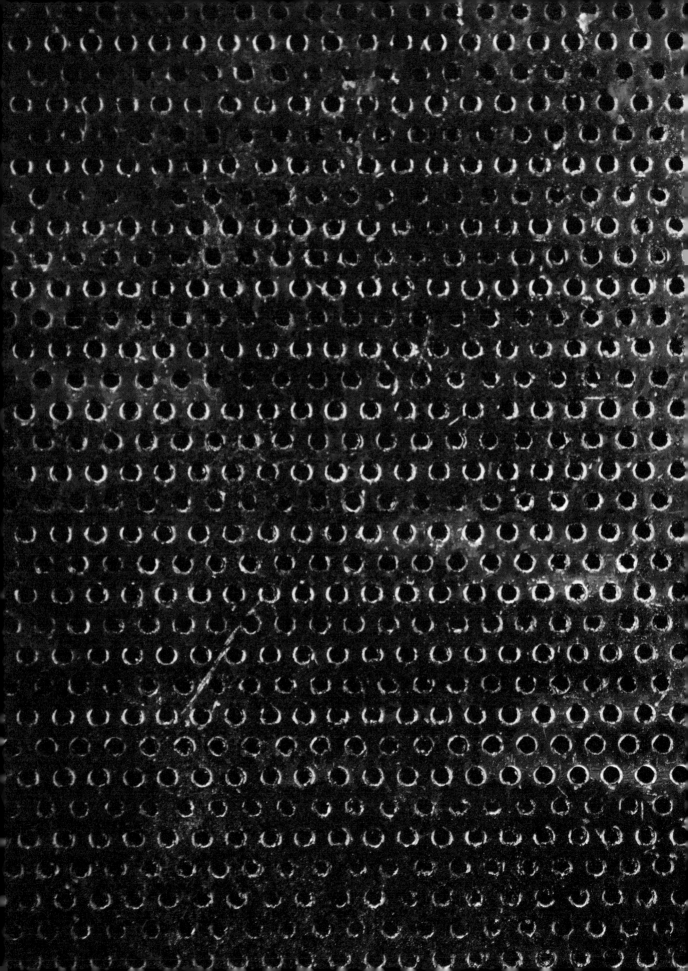

| DOUBLE-CRUST PIES |

CLASSIC APPLE PIE

Baking an apple pie is so rewarding because there are so many different varieties of apples available with differing harvest times. You can get good apples from late summer well into winter. Apples can also be stored for a long time provided they are kept cold.

The choice of apples for this pie affects both the flavor and the consistency. I prefer using apples that are firmer and more acidic for baking; for example, Ingrid Marie or Aroma, which are Swedish varieties, or Cortland or Golden Delicious work well.

1 pie, 8 inches in diameter, 8–10 servings

PIECRUST

2¼ cups all-purpose flour

2½ tablespoons granulated sugar

¼ teaspoon sea salt

½ teaspoon ground cinnamon

1¼ cups (9¾ ounces) cold butter

5–7 tablespoons ice-cold water

APPLE FILLING

3½ pounds apples

2 tablespoons butter

6 tablespoons granulated sugar

¼ cup light Muscovado sugar (firmly packed in measuring cup)

2 tablespoons freshly squeezed lemon juice

1¼ teaspoons ground cinnamon

½ teaspoon vanilla extract

¼ teaspoon sea salt

2 tablespoons all-purpose flour

2 tablespoons cornstarch

2 teaspoons all-purpose flour

2 teaspoons granulated sugar (to sprinkle over bottom crust)

GLAZE

1 egg

1 tablespoon milk

Pinch of sea salt

1 tablespoon Turbinado or raw cane sugar

PIECRUST

1. Mix the flour, granulated sugar, salt, and cinnamon in a bowl. Dice the butter and add it to the flour. Use your fingers to pinch the butter into the flour until the dough is crumbly.
2. Add the cold water gradually and mix it in with a fork. If the dough coheres when pressed together, it has enough water.
3. Flatten the dough somewhat and cover it completely with plastic wrap. Refrigerate the dough for at least 1 hour, preferably overnight.

APPLE FILLING

1. Peel, core, and slice the apples.
2. Melt the butter in a saucepan large enough to hold all the apples. Add the apples, granulated sugar, Muscovado sugar, lemon juice, cinnamon, vanilla extract, and salt. Mix the ingredients, stirring carefully. Bring the mixture to a boil and then simmer it over low heat for 4 to 5 minutes or until the apples have softened and begun releasing their liquid. Stir occasionally.
3. Sprinkle in the 2 tablespoons of flour and the cornstarch, stir, and continue simmering for another 2 minutes, until the liquid has thickened slightly. Remove the saucepan from the heat and let the apple mixture cool completely.

ROLLING OUT THE CRUST AND BAKING THE PIE

1. Preheat the oven to 435°F.
2. On a floured work surface, roll out a little more than half of the dough until it's about ⅛ inch thick. Lay this bottom crust in the pie pan and refrigerate it.
3. Roll out the rest of the dough until it's about 11 inches in diameter; cut it into strips with a knife or pizza cutter.
4. Remove the pie shell from the refrigerator. Mix the 2 teaspoons of flour and 2 teaspoons of sugar in a small bowl and sprinkle it over the bottom crust. Add the apple mixture. Brush the edges with water. Weave a lattice top with the dough strips (see page 16). Cut away any excess overhang, leaving about 1¼ inches all around, and decorate with a fork or method of your choice (see page 18). Otherwise, cut away the overhang, leaving a narrow rim. Place the pie in the freezer for 15 minutes.
5. To make the glaze, whisk the egg, milk, and salt in a small bowl. Remove the pie from the freezer and glaze brush it with this mixture, and then sprinkle the Turbinado sugar on top.
6. Bake the pie on the lower rack of the oven for 20 minutes. Reduce the temperature to 350°F and bake it for another 40 minutes, until the filling is bubbly. If the piecrust looks like it is becoming too dark toward the end of the baking time, cover the top crust—or only the edges, as necessary—with aluminum foil or parchment paper. Remove the pie from the oven and let it cool completely. Serve with Caramel Ice Cream (page 137), if desired.

BLUEBERRY PIE WITH BUTTERMILK AND LEMON

Buttermilk is the liquid that remains after churning butter. It is similar to sour milk but has a thinner consistency. The acidic flavor goes perfectly with lemon and blueberries. If you can't find buttermilk in your grocery store, you can make a substitute: Mix ⅔ cup of milk with 2 tablespoons of freshly squeezed lemon juice and let it sit for 10 minutes. The milk will curdle, and then it's ready to use.

3 small pies, about 5¼ inches in diameter, 6–8 servings

PIECRUST

2 cups all-purpose flour
2 tablespoons granulated sugar
¼ teaspoon sea salt
16 tablespoons (8 ounces) cold butter
6–8 tablespoons cold buttermilk

BLUEBERRY FILLING

1½ pounds blueberries, fresh or frozen
6–8 tablespoons granulated sugar
Finely grated zest of 1 lemon
½ teaspoon vanilla extract
4 tablespoons cornstarch
4 tablespoons freshly squeezed lemon juice

GLAZE

1 egg
1 tablespoon milk
Pinch of sea salt
1 tablespoon Turbinado or raw cane sugar

PIECRUST

1. Mix the flour, granulated sugar, and salt in a bowl. Dice the butter and add it to the flour. Use your fingers to pinch the butter into the flour until the dough is crumbly.
2. Add the cold buttermilk (begin with the smaller amount and gradually add more if the dough feels too dry) and mix it in with a fork. If you pick up a bit of the dough and it coheres when pressed together, it has enough liquid.
3. Lay a piece of plastic wrap over the dough, flatten the dough somewhat, and then cover the dough completely with plastic wrap. Refrigerate the dough for at least 1 hour, preferably overnight.

BLUEBERRY FILLING

1. Mix the blueberries, granulated sugar, lemon zest, and vanilla extract together in a saucepan. Bring the mixture to a boil. In a small cup, dissolve the cornstarch in the lemon juice and pour it into the blueberry mixture, stirring as you pour. Simmer the filling for a few minutes, stirring constantly until it thickens.
2. Remove the filling from the heat and let it cool completely.

ROLLING OUT THE CRUST AND BAKING THE PIES

1. Preheat the oven to 400°F.
2. Divide the piecrust dough into three equal pieces and roll them out one at a time on a floured surface until they are ⅛ inch thick. Cut out dough circles to fit the pans (for a pan 5¼ inches in diameter, the circles should measure about 8¼ inches in diameter). Set the remaining scraps aside. Lay the bottom crusts in the pans and refrigerate them.
3. Roll out the dough scraps and cut them into strips or shapes with a knife, pizza cutter, or scissors.
4. Remove the pie shells from the refrigerator. Add the filling. If making a lattice-top crust, brush the edges with a little water. Weave a lattice top with the dough strips and prepare the edge as you like or lay the piecrust shapes on top of the filling and press down slightly.
5. Freeze the pies for 15 minutes (so they hold their shape better).
6. To make the glaze, whisk the egg, milk, and salt in a small bowl. Glaze the lattice top with the egg mixture and then sprinkle the Turbinado sugar on top. If using small shapes of dough on top, there is no need to add the egg wash.
7. Bake the pies on the lower rack of the oven for 20 minutes. Reduce the temperature to 350°F and bake for another 25 to 30 minutes, or until the pies are golden and the filling is bubbly. Let the pies cool completely. Serve them with Vanilla Ice Cream (page 139) or Vanilla Sauce (page 138), if desired.

PEACH AND STRAWBERRY PIE WITH BROWN BUTTER

The dough for this piecrust will be quite hard after being refrigerated, so take it out well ahead of time. Alternatively, you can cheat as I usually do and heat it on low in the microwave for just a few seconds at a time. It should absolutely not be too warm, as that will make it difficult to roll out.

1 pie, approximately 8 inches in diameter, 8–10 servings

PIECRUST

1¼ cups (9¾ ounces) unsalted butter

2¼ cups all-purpose flour

2 tablespoons light Muscovado sugar (firmly packed in measuring spoon)

½ teaspoon sea salt

½ teaspoon vanilla extract

6–9 tablespoons ice-cold water

PEACH AND STRAWBERRY FILLING

2 pounds peaches

14 ounces strawberries (preferably fresh)

½ cup light Muscovado sugar (firmly packed in measuring cup)

½ teaspoon ground cinnamon

2 tablespoons freshly squeezed lemon juice

3 tablespoons cornstarch

GLAZE

1 egg

1 tablespoon milk

Pinch of sea salt

1 tablespoon Turbinado or raw cane sugar

PIECRUST

1. Heat the butter in a saucepan over medium heat. Stirring occasionally, let the butter simmer for a few minutes, until small brown spots appear in the bottom of the pan and the butter smells nutty. Remove the pan from the heat and cool the butter slightly. Pour the butter into silicon ice cube trays (or into a parchment-lined pan). Freeze the butter cubes for 20 to 30 minutes, until the butter is cold and firm.

2. Mix the flour, Muscovado sugar, salt, and vanilla extract in a bowl. Add the frozen butter cubes to the flour mixture. Use your fingers to pinch the butter into the flour until the dough is crumbly.

3. Add the cold water (begin with the smaller amount and gradually add more if the dough feels too dry) and mix it in with a fork. If you pick up a bit of the dough and it coheres when pressed together, it has enough water.

4. Lay a piece of plastic wrap over the dough, flatten the dough somewhat, and then cover the dough completely with plastic wrap. Refrigerate the dough for at least 1 hour, preferably overnight.

PEACH AND STRAWBERRY FILLING

1. Halve the peaches, remove the pits, and slice the fruit. Hull the strawberries and halve or quarter them, depending on their size. Pour all the fruit into a large bowl and mix in the Muscovado sugar, cinnamon, lemon juice, and cornstarch. Let the fruit stand at room temperature for 20 minutes.

2. Place a sieve over a large saucepan and pour in the fruit so the liquid can drain. Put the fruit back in the bowl. Bring the liquid to a boil, constantly whisking with a hand whisk. Simmer for about 1 minute, until the liquid has thickened slightly. It should be a little thicker than originally but not as thick as cream. Pour the liquid into the bowl with the fruit. Let the fruit and liquid cool.

ROLLING OUT THE CRUST AND BAKING THE PIE

1. Preheat the oven to 435°F.

2. Remove the dough from the refrigerator and leave it at room temperature for about 15 minutes to make it easier to roll out. On a floured work surface, roll out a little more than half of the dough until it's about ⅛ inch thick. Lay this bottom crust in the pie pan and refrigerate it.

3. Roll out the rest of the dough into a large circle that will cover the top of the pie.

»»*The recipe continues on page 37.*««

4. Take the pie shell out of the refrigerator and pour in the filling. Brush the edge with a little water. Lay the top crust over the filling and press it down with your fingers. Cut away any overhang, leaving about 1¼ inches all around if you want a decorative edge. Save the leftover dough for cutting out some leaves.

5. To make the glaze, whisk the egg, milk, and salt in a small bowl. Brush the bottoms of the dough leaves with a little of the egg mixture and arrange them on the top crust. Put the pie in the freezer for 15 minutes (to help it hold its shape better in the oven while baking).

6. Remove the pie from the freezer and glaze it with the remaining egg mixture. Sprinkle the Turbinado sugar on top. Use a knife to make a few slits in the top crust.

7. Bake the pie on the lower rack of the oven for 15 minutes. Reduce the temperature to 350°F and bake for another 35 to 45 minutes, until the edges are golden brown. If the crust darkens too much toward the end of the baking time, cover it with aluminum foil or parchment paper. Remove the pie from the oven and let it cool completely. Serve with Vanilla Ice Cream (page 139), if desired.

PEACH PIE WITH COGNAC

This peach pie is unbelievably good and was baked numerous times while I created this book. It's a clear favorite, particularly with a big scoop of ice cream.

1 pie, approximately 8 inches in diameter, 6–8 servings

PIECRUST
1¾ cups all-purpose flour
2 tablespoons light Muscovado sugar (firmly packed in measuring spoon)
¼ teaspoon sea salt
14 tablespoons (6 ounces) cold butter
3–4 tablespoons cognac
1–2 tablespoons ice-cold water (if more liquid is needed)

PEACH FILLING
1½ pounds peaches
2 tablespoons cornstarch
½ teaspoon ground cinnamon
⅓ cup light Muscovado sugar (firmly packed in measuring cup)
1 tablespoon cognac
¼ teaspoon sea salt
2 tablespoons butter

GLAZE
1 egg
1 tablespoon milk
Pinch of sea salt
1 tablespoon Turbinado or raw cane sugar

TIP: It is not always easy to remove the pits from peaches without mashing the fruit. The trick is to start at the beginning, by picking out fruit that is slightly soft but not mushy. Usually it is the hard fruit that has the pits firmly embedded. If I don't succeed in removing the pit, I usually slice the fruit around it. It doesn't always make the prettiest slices, but what does that matter? What's important is that it tastes good.

PIECRUST
1. Mix the flour, Muscovado sugar, and salt in a bowl. Dice the butter and add it to the flour mixture. Use your fingers to pinch in the butter until the dough is crumbly.
2. Add the cognac and mix it in with a fork. If you pick up a bit of the dough and it coheres when pressed together, it has enough liquid. If the dough seems a little dry, add some of the water.
3. Lay a piece of plastic wrap over the dough, flatten the dough somewhat, and then cover the dough completely with plastic wrap. Refrigerate the dough for at least 1 hour, preferably overnight.

PEACH FILLING
1. Halve the peaches, remove the pits, and slice the fruit. Put the fruit in a bowl and mix in the cornstarch and cinnamon.
2. Mix the Muscovado sugar and the cognac in a small saucepan. Stir until the sugar dissolves and then bring the liquid to a boil. Simmer the mixture for 1 minute, carefully stirring now and then. Add the salt and butter and stir until the butter has melted. Pour the mixture over the peaches and mix them well. Let the filling cool completely.

ROLLING OUT THE CRUST AND BAKING THE PIE
1. Preheat the oven to 435°F.
2. Roll out a little more than half the dough on a floured work surface until ⅛ inch thick. Lay this bottom crust in the pan and refrigerate it.
3. Roll out the rest of the dough and cut it into strips of various widths, using a knife or pizza cutter.
4. Remove the pie shell from the refrigerator. Pour the peach filling into the pie shell and brush the edge of the crust with a little water. Weave a lattice with the dough strips (see page 16). Fold any overhang up along the edges and make a decorative edge using your fingers (see page 18).
5. Put the pie in the freezer for 15 minutes (to help it hold its shape better in the oven while baking).
6. To make the glaze, whisk the egg, milk, and salt in a small bowl. Brush the pie dough with the egg mixture and sprinkle the Turbinado sugar on top.
7. Bake the pie on the lower rack of the oven for 15 minutes. Reduce the temperature to 350°F and bake for another 40 to 45 minutes, until the piecrust is golden brown and the filling is bubbly. If the crust darkens too much toward the end of the baking time, cover it with aluminum foil or parchment paper. Remove the pie from the oven and let it cool completely. Serve it with Vanilla Ice Cream (page 137), if desired.

CHERRY PIE WITH ALMONDS

Almonds and cherries are a classic combination. In this case, I used almond flour for the pie dough. You can use either fresh or frozen cherries. With frozen cherries the filling will have a little more liquid, but on the other hand, the cherries are usually pitted, which is practical when you don't have a lot of time.

1 pie, approximately 7 inches in diameter, 6–8 servings

PIECRUST

1⅓ cups all-purpose flour
⅔ cup almond flour (2 ounces)
2 tablespoons granulated sugar
¼ teaspoon sea salt
14 tablespoons (6 ounces) cold butter
3–5 tablespoons ice-cold water

CHERRY FILLING

About 1½ pounds (26½ ounces) pitted cherries (approximately 2 pounds/31¾ ounces unpitted whole cherries)
6 tablespoons granulated sugar
¼ teaspoon sea salt
½ teaspoon vanilla extract
1 tablespoon Kirsch (cherry liqueur, optional)
2 tablespoons cornstarch
2 tablespoons freshly squeezed lemon juice

GLAZE

1 egg
1 tablespoon milk
Pinch of sea salt
1 tablespoon Turbinado or raw cane sugar

PIECRUST

1. Mix the all-purpose flour, almond flour, granulated sugar, and salt in a bowl. Dice the butter and add it to the flour mixture. Use your fingers to pinch in the butter until the dough is crumbly.
2. Add the cold water (begin with the smaller amount and gradually add more if the dough feels too dry) and mix it in with a fork. When you pick up a bit of the dough and it coheres when pressed together, it has enough water.
3. Lay a piece of plastic wrap over the dough, flatten the dough somewhat, and then cover the dough completely with plastic wrap. Refrigerate it for at least 1 hour, preferably overnight.

CHERRY FILLING

1. Mix the cherries, granulated sugar, salt, vanilla extract, and Kirsch in a saucepan. Bring the mixture to a boil and then simmer it over low heat for 3 to 4 minutes or until the cherries begin to soften.
2. In a small cup, dissolve the cornstarch in the lemon juice and pour it into the saucepan, stirring as you add it in. Let the mixture simmer for another minute, or until thickened. Let it cool completely.

ROLLING OUT THE CRUST AND BAKING THE PIE

1. Preheat the oven to 435°F.
2. On a lightly floured work surface, roll a little more than half the dough into a large circle, ⅛ inch thick. Lay this bottom crust in the pan and refrigerate the pie shell.
3. Roll the rest of the dough into a large circle. Using a round piping tip or a thimble, cut out small holes in the dough.
4. Take the pie shell out of the refrigerator, add the filling, and brush the edge with a little water. Lay the top crust over the pie and press it down around the edge. Cut away any excess dough if you don't want to make a decorative edge, but leave a narrow rim on the edge of the pie plate so it doesn't shrink in too much.
5. Put the pie in the freezer for 15 minutes (to help it hold its shape better in the oven while baking).
6. To make the glaze, whisk the egg, milk, and salt in a small bowl. Brush the crust with the egg mixture and sprinkle the Turbinado sugar on top.
7. Bake the pie on the lower rack of the oven for 15 minutes. Reduce the temperature to 350°F and bake for another 45 minutes, until the piecrust is golden brown and the filling bubbly. If the crust darkens too much toward the end of the baking time, cover it with aluminum foil or parchment paper. Remove the pie from the oven and let it cool completely before you cut it, so the filling will set better. Serve it with Vanilla Ice Cream (page 137), if desired.

PLUM PIE WITH PISTACHIOS, RUM, AND VANILLA

Making a piecrust dough with a mixture of all-purpose flour and nuts is always a winner. The dough might be somewhat brittle to work with, but at the same time, it will be unbelievably fine and have a mild, nutty flavor when it is baked.

1 pie, approximately 8 inches in diameter, 8–10 servings

PIECRUST

2 ounces shelled pistachios (about 6 tablespoons unshelled nuts), dry-roasted and unsalted

1⅓ cups all-purpose flour

1 tablespoon granulated sugar

¼ teaspoon sea salt

14 tablespoons (6 ounces) cold butter

3–5 tablespoons ice-cold water

PLUM FILLING

2 pounds plums

½ cup granulated sugar

¼ teaspoon sea salt

3 tablespoons cornstarch

1 teaspoon vanilla extract

1–2 tablespoons dark rum (optional)

PISTACHIO CRUMBLE

1 ounce shelled pistachios (about ¼ cup unshelled nuts), dry-roasted and unsalted

2½ tablespoons all-purpose flour

2 tablespoons granulated sugar

½ teaspoon ground cinnamon

1½ tablespoons (¾ ounce) cold butter

GLAZE

1 egg

1 tablespoon milk

Pinch of sea salt

1 tablespoon Turbinado or raw cane sugar

PIECRUST

1. Grind the pistachio nuts to a relatively fine meal. Mix the ground nuts with the flour, granulated sugar, and salt in a bowl. Dice the butter and add it to the flour mixture. Use your fingers to pinch the butter into the flour mixture until the dough is crumbly.
2. Add the cold water (begin with the smaller amount and gradually add more if the dough feels too dry) and mix it in with a fork. If you pick up a bit of the dough and it coheres when pressed together, it has enough water.
3. Lay a piece of plastic wrap over the dough, flatten the dough somewhat, and then cover it completely with plastic wrap. Refrigerate the dough for at least 1 hour, preferably overnight.

PLUM FILLING

1. Remove the pits from the plums and slice them. Place the pitted plums in a bowl.
2. Mix the granulated sugar, salt, cornstarch, and vanilla extract in a small bowl and then add the mixture to the plums. Let the filling stand at room temperature for 20 minutes.
3. Place a sieve over a large saucepan and pour in the plums to drain the liquid. Put the plums back in the bowl. Bring the liquid to a boil, stirring constantly with a hand whisk; add the rum, if desired. Simmer the mixture for about 1 minute or until the liquid has slightly thickened. Pour the liquid into the bowl with the plums. Let the filling cool.

PISTACHIO CRUMBLE

1. In a food processor, grind the pistachios to a relatively fine meal.
2. Add the flour, granulated sugar, cinnamon, and butter and pulse until crumbly.
3. Refrigerate the mixture while you prepare the rest of the pie.

ROLLING OUT THE CRUST AND BAKING THE PIE

1. Preheat the oven to 435°F. Remove the piecrust dough from the refrigerator and roll out a little more than half of it on a floured work surface until it's ⅛ inch thick. Lay this bottom crust in the pie pan. Fold the overhang under and crimp it with your fingers (page 18). Refrigerate the shell while you prepare the rest of the pie. Roll out the rest of the dough and cut strips that you can braid. The braids should be long enough to cover the top of the pie.

»»The recipe continues on the next page. »»

2. Take the shell out of the refrigerator and brush the edges where you will attach the braids with a little water. Add alternate layers of the filling and the pistachio crumble in the pie shell, ending with a layer of the crumble. Make the braids and press them in well at the edge of the shell. Put the pie in the freezer for 15 minutes (to help it hold its shape better in the oven while baking).
3. Whisk the egg, milk, and salt in a small bowl. Brush the pie dough with the egg mixture and sprinkle the Turbinado sugar on top.
4. Bake the pie on the lower rack of the oven for 20 minutes. Reduce the temperature to 350°F and bake it for another 30 to 35 minutes, until the piecrust is golden brown and the filling bubbly. If the crust darkens too much toward the end of the baking time, cover it with aluminum foil or parchment paper. Remove the pie from the oven and let it cool completely before you cut it, so the filling will set better. Serve the pie with Vanilla Ice Cream (page 137), if desired.

RHUBARB SLAB PIE

Who says that a pie has to be round and baked in a pie pan? This recipe is totally uncomplicated, which is excellent for baking when you can't manage all the bother with shaping. The top of the pie leaves a lot of room for creativity, something I very much appreciate. Make some fun decorations with the leftover dough.

12 pieces

PIECRUST

1¼ cups all-purpose flour

1 tablespoon granulated sugar

¼ teaspoon sea salt

¼ teaspoon ground cardamom

9 tablespoons (4½ ounces) cold butter

3 tablespoons crème fraîche

3–5 tablespoons ice-cold water

RHUBARB FILLING

18 ounces rhubarb

½ cup granulated sugar

½ teaspoon ground cardamom

¼ teaspoon sea salt

Finely grated zest of ½ lemon

2 tablespoons cornstarch

1 tablespoon freshly squeezed lemon juice

GLAZE

1 egg

1 tablespoon milk

Pinch of sea salt

1 tablespoon Turbinado or raw cane sugar

PIECRUST

1. Mix the flour, granulated sugar, salt, and cardamom in a bowl. Dice the butter and add it to the flour mixture. Use your fingers to pinch in the butter until the dough is crumbly.
2. Add the crème fraîche and water (gradually add more if the dough feels too dry) and mix it in with a fork. If you pick up a bit of the dough and it coheres when pressed together, it has enough liquid. Lay a piece of plastic wrap over the dough, flatten the dough somewhat, and then cover the dough completely with plastic wrap. Refrigerate the dough for at least 1 hour, preferably overnight.

RHUBARB FILLING

1. Cut the rhubarb into small pieces. Put the rhubarb in a saucepan and mix in the granulated sugar, cardamom, salt, and lemon zest.
2. Cook the mixture until it releases some liquid and then simmer it for 2 to 3 minutes, until the rhubarb has softened a little.
3. In a small cup, dissolve the cornstarch in the lemon juice and then stir it into the rhubarb mixture. Simmer for about 1 minute, until slightly thickened. Remove the saucepan from the heat and let the mixture cool.

ROLLING OUT THE CRUST AND BAKING THE PIE

1. Preheat the oven to 400°F.
2. On a floured work surface, roll out a little less than half the dough to a large rectangle, about 10¾ x 15¾ inches and ⅛ inch thick. Transfer the dough to a cutting board or a baking sheet lined with parchment paper. Roll the rest of the dough the same way, making a slightly larger rectangle.
3. Pour the rhubarb mixture onto the smaller rectangle, leaving about 1½ inches on all sides free of filling. Brush the edges of the dough with water.
4. Place the larger rectangle on top, pressing it down all around the edges. Trim the edges with a knife or pizza cutter to even them out. Make a pattern around the edge using a fork. Place the pie in the freezer for 15 minutes (to help it hold its shape better in the oven while baking). Cut out some small stars with the leftover dough.
5. Take the pie out of the freezer and, if it's on a cutting board, place it on a baking sheet lined with parchment paper.
6. To make the glaze, whisk the egg, milk, and salt together in a small bowl. Brush the pie with the egg mixture, arrange the little stars on the top crust, and sprinkle the Turbinado sugar on top. Cut a few slits in the top crust. Bake the pie on the lower rack of the oven for 15 minutes. Reduce the temperature to 350°F and bake for another 25 to 30 minutes, until the piecrust is golden brown. Remove the pie from the oven and let it cool completely. Serve with Vanilla Ice Cream (page 137) or Whipped Honey Crème Fraîche (page 141), if desired.

CINNAMON ROLL PIE WITH APPLES

This apple pie is absolutely wonderful for anyone who loves cinnamon buns. And apple pie. And dulce de leche. This pie is a little more time-consuming to make than the other pies in this book, but I think it is totally worth the effort. If you want to bake the pie without the cinnamon rolls on the top crust, just roll out the dough as is. In that case, add an extra teaspoon of cinnamon to the filling.

1 pie, approximately 8 inches in diameter, 8–10 servings

PIECRUST

2¼ cups all-purpose flour

3 tablespoons granulated sugar

¼ teaspoon sea salt

16 tablespoons (8 ounces) cold butter

5–7 tablespoons ice-cold water

APPLE FILLING

2¾ pounds apples

2 tablespoons (1 ounce) butter

¾ cup dulce de leche

½ teaspoon ground cinnamon

¼ teaspoon sea salt

4 tablespoons cornstarch

3 tablespoons freshly squeezed orange juice

CRUST FILLING

5¼ tablespoons (2⅔ ounces) butter, at room temperature

1 tablespoon ground cinnamon

1 teaspoon ground cardamom

GLAZE

1 egg

1 tablespoon milk

Pinch of sea salt

1–2 tablespoons pearl sugar, Turbinado, or raw cane sugar

PIE CRUST

1. Mix the flour, granulated sugar, and salt in a bowl. Dice the butter and add it to the flour mixture. Use your fingers to pinch in the butter until the dough is crumbly.
2. Add the water (begin with the smaller amount and gradually add more if the dough feels too dry) and mix it in with a fork. If you pick up a bit of the dough and it coheres when pressed together, it has enough water.
3. Lay a piece of plastic wrap over the dough, flatten the dough somewhat, and then cover the dough completely with plastic wrap. Refrigerate the dough for at least 1 hour, preferably overnight.

APPLE FILLING

1. Peel and core the apples. Cut them into thin slices and place them in a large bowl.
2. Melt the butter in a large saucepan. Add the apple slices and sauté them for 2 to 3 minutes, until the apples soften slightly. Carefully stir occasionally.
3. Add the dulce de leche, cinnamon, and salt. In a small cup, dissolve the cornstarch in the orange juice and stir it into the saucepan. Let the mixture simmer over low heat as you stir for a few more minutes, until the mixture has thickened. Let the filling cool completely.

ROLLING OUT THE CRUST AND BAKING THE PIE

1. Preheat the oven to 435°F.
2. For the crust filling, mix the butter with the cinnamon and cardamom. Take the dough out of the refrigerator and divide it into two equal pieces. On a floured work surface, roll out one half of the dough into a rectangle about 15¾ x 13¾ inches. Spread this dough with half of the butter mixture and roll up the dough from the long side. Repeat with the other half of the dough and the remainder of the crust filling. Place the rolls on a cutting board and then in the freezer for 5 to 10 minutes.
3. Remove one roll from the freezer and cut it into ⅔-inch slices (just as if you were preparing cinnamon buns). Fill a pie pan with the slices, covering the bottom and sides (the pieces should have a little space between them). Press the slices together so they form a pie shell. Transfer the pie pan to the freezer.
4. Take the other roll out of the freezer and slice it in the same way, but arrange the slices in a circle (large enough to cover the top of the pan) on parchment paper and then roll them out a little to firm up the circle. If the slices don't want to cohere, you can brush a little water between them. If it is difficult to roll the slices together, press them together.

»»*The recipe continues on page 50.*»»

5. Take the pie shell out of the freezer and pour in the apple filling. Brush the edge with a little water and add the top crust. It is easiest to leave the crust on the parchment paper and fold it out over the pie filling, then remove the parchment. Cut away any overhang, leaving a rim about 1¼ inches wide all around if you want to make a decorative edge. Put the pie in the freezer for 15 minutes (to help it hold its shape better in the oven while baking).

6. Remove the pie from the freezer. To make the glaze, whisk the egg, milk, and salt in a small bowl. Brush the pie dough with the egg mixture and sprinkle the pearl sugar on top.

7. Bake the pie on the lower rack of the oven for 10 minutes. Reduce the temperature to 350°F and bake for another 45 to 50 minutes, until the piecrust is golden brown. Remove the pie from the oven and let it cool completely. Serve the pie with Vanilla Ice Cream (page 137), if desired.

NUT AND CARAMEL PIE

These nut and caramel pies are fantastically good for anyone who loves the combination of nuts and caramel. You can use whatever nuts you want here, so choose your favorites.

4 small pies, 4¼ x 2¾ inches, 6–8 servings

PIECRUST

1 ounce hazelnuts

1¼ cups all-purpose flour

3 tablespoons granulated sugar

¼ teaspoon sea salt

12 tablespoons (5¼ ounces) butter

NUT AND CARAMEL FILLING

1¾ cups mixed tree nuts, such as hazelnuts, sweet almonds, pecans, and cashews

7 tablespoons (3½ ounces) butter

⅓ cup light Muscovado sugar (firmly packed in measuring cup)

¼ cup honey

2 tablespoons whipping cream

¼ teaspoon sea salt

PIECRUST

1. Preheat the oven to 350°F.
2. In a processor, grind the hazelnuts to a fine meal. Mix the hazelnut meal with the all-purpose flour, granulated sugar, and salt. Melt the butter and blend it into the flour mixture. Use your fingers to pinch the mixture into a dough.
3. Divide three-fourths of the dough into four pieces to fill four small, rectangular pie forms. Press the dough into the bottom and sides of each pan and prick the crust all over with a fork. Cover the rest of the dough with plastic wrap and refrigerate it while you prepare the filling.
4. Blind-bake the pie shells (see page 24) on the lower rack of the oven for 22 to 23 minutes, until the crusts just start to brown on the bottom. Remove the pie shells from the oven and let them cool.

PREPARING THE FILLING, ROLLING OUT THE CRUST, AND BAKING THE PIE

1. To begin preparing the filling, toast the nuts on a baking sheet or in an ovenproof pan on the middle rack of the oven for 8 to 10 minutes, only until they just start to change color. (If you are using hazelnuts in their skins, lay them on a kitchen towel and rub them with the towel to remove most of the skins.) Let the nuts cool and then chop them coarsely.
2. Roll out the remaining one-fourth of the dough between two pieces of parchment paper (the dough is fragile and might otherwise fall apart). Cut the dough into strips or cut out stars or another shape.
3. To finish making the filling, mix the butter, Muscovado sugar, honey, cream, and salt in a saucepan. Stir as you bring the mixture to a boil over medium heat. Stir in the chopped, toasted nuts and remove the saucepan from the heat.
4. Let the nut filling cool a little (but not completely, or the nuts will then be too hard) and divide it among the four pie shells. Garnish the tops with dough strips or shapes.
5. Place the pies on a baking sheet lined with parchment paper and bake them on the lower rack of the oven for 25 to 30 minutes, until the filing is golden brown and bubbly. Remove the pies from the oven and let them cool completely. A little lightly whipped cream tops off these pies well.

| CRUMBLE-TOPPED PIES |

FOREST BERRY CRUMBLE PIE

I usually throw this good crumble pie together when the berries in the freezer have begun to sing their last verse. Sometimes it has a mixture of just about everything possible. Most often it has blackberries, blueberries, and raspberries because they grow plentifully near where I live, and I usually have a supply of them in the freezer.

Baking soda gives the crumble dough more of a shortcrust-pastry quality, but it can be omitted for a more traditional crispy crumble.

It's great to have a lot of the crumble on the pie because it is so good. If you think it is too much, you can always freeze any extra to save for another occasion. The frozen dough crumbles do not need to be thawed—just spread them out on top of the berries.

1 pie, about 8 inches in diameter, 6–8 servings

CRUMBLE TOPPING

¾ cup rolled oats

¾ cup all-purpose flour

6 tablespoons coarse sugar

¼ teaspoon baking soda

¼ teaspoon sea salt

9 tablespoons (4½ ounces) butter, at room temperature

FOREST BERRY FILLING

21 ounces mixed berries (for example, raspberries, blueberries, blackberries), fresh or frozen

6 tablespoons coarse sugar

2 tablespoons cornstarch

½ teaspoon vanilla extract

CRUMBLE TOPPING

1. Mix the oats, flour, sugar, baking soda, and salt in a bowl.
2. Add the butter and pinch it in with your fingers until the dough is crumbly. Place the bowl in the refrigerator while you prepare the filling.

PREPARING THE FILLING AND ASSEMBLING AND BAKING THE PIE

1. Preheat the oven to 400°F.
2. To make the filling, pour the berries into a large bowl and mix in the sugar, cornstarch, and vanilla extract. Stir gently to blend the ingredients.
3. Pour the berry mixture into a pie dish. (*Note:* Do not use a springform pan, as the liquid will leak out.) Crumble the topping evenly over the filling.
4. Bake the pie on the middle rack of the oven for 35 to 40 minutes or until the topping is golden brown and the filling is bubbly. Remove the pie from the oven and let it cool. Serve it with Vanilla Sauce (page 138) or Vanilla Cream (page 139), if desired.

APPLE CRUMBLE PIE WITH HONEY AND PECANS

I baked this apple crumble pie for the first time for a wine tasting that I held together with my friend Lua. She chose the wines and I baked foods to go with them. She had chosen a wine that complemented apples and nuts, and then I decided to improvise this pie. The participants loved it so much (as did I) that, of course, it had to have a place in this book.

1 pie, about 8 inches in diameter, 6–8 servings

CRUMBLE TOPPING
¾ cup all-purpose flour
½ cup coarse sugar
¼ teaspoon ground cinnamon
¼ teaspoon sea salt
3½ ounces pecans
6½ tablespoons (3¼ ounces) cold butter

APPLE AND HONEY FILLING
30 ounces apples (about 4 apples)
⅓ cup honey
2 tablespoons cornstarch

CRUMBLE TOPPING
Mix all the ingredients except the butter in a food processor or blender and pulse it to a relatively fine meal. Cut the butter into small pieces and add it to the flour mixture. Pulse the mixture until the dough is crumbly.

PREPARING THE FILLING AND ASSEMBLING AND BAKING THE PIE
1. Preheat the oven to 350°F.
2. To prepare the filling, peel, core, and slice the apples. Put the slices in a large bowl and add the honey and cornstarch.
3. Pour the apple filling into a pie pan. (*Note*: Do not use a springform pan, as the liquid will leak out.) Crumble the topping evenly over the filling. Bake the pie on the middle rack of the oven for 40 to 45 minutes or until the topping is golden brown and the filling is bubbly. Remove the pie from the oven and let it cool. Serve the pie with Caramel Ice Cream (page 137) or Caramel Vanilla Sauce (page 138), if desired.

CRUMBLE PIE WITH BROWN BUTTER, CHOCOLATE, AND BLACKBERRIES

The combination of blackberries and chocolate is not very common, and usually raspberries are considered the perfect taste pairing. But I must say that the mild flavor and acidity of blackberries offers a more enjoyable taste experience with chocolate.

4 pies, 4¼ inches in diameter, 4 servings

CRUMBLE TOPPING
7 tablespoons (3½ ounces) unsalted butter
1 cup all-purpose flour
⅓ cup rolled oats
⅓ cup granulated sugar
¼ teaspoon sea salt
1 tablespoon cocoa
2⅔ ounces chopped dark chocolate or chocolate chips (70% cacao)

BLACKBERRY FILLING
1 pound blackberries, fresh or frozen
2 tablespoons cornstarch
¼ cup granulated sugar
¼ teaspoon sea salt
½ teaspoon vanilla extract

CRUMBLE TOPPING
1. Heat the butter in a saucepan over medium heat. Let the butter simmer for a few minutes, until brown spots appear on the bottom of the pan and the butter smells nutty; stir occasionally. Remove the pan from the heat and pour the butter into a bowl. Place the bowl in the refrigerator or freezer until the butter begins to firm up a little, to the consistency of softened butter. Keep an eye on it!
2. Mix the flour, oats, sugar, salt, and cocoa in a bowl. Mix in the brown butter and pinch the dough together until crumbly. Add the chocolate.

PREPARING THE FILLING AND ASSEMBLING THE PIE
1. Preheat the oven to 350°F.
2. To make the filling, pour the blackberries into a large bowl and mix in the cornstarch, sugar, salt, and vanilla extract.
3. Divide the blackberry mixture evenly into the little pie pans (*Note:* Do not use a springform pan, as the liquid will leak out.) Crumble the topping evenly over the filling.
4. Bake the pies on the middle rack of the oven for 35 minutes or until the filling is bubbly. Remove the pies from the oven and let them cool. Serve with Vanilla Ice Cream (page 137), if desired.

RED CURRANT PIE WITH WHITE CHOCOLATE

This pie is unbelievably easy, sticky, and slightly tart, and you can readily toss it together in a few minutes. If you would rather make a large pie instead of several small ones, that, of course, is just fine.

6 pies, 4 inches in diameter, 6 servings

CRUMBLE TOPPING

¾ cup all-purpose flour

6 tablespoons granulated sugar

¾ teaspoon baking powder

¼ teaspoon sea salt

½ teaspoon vanilla extract

9 tablespoons (4½ ounces) butter, at room temperature

2⅔ ounces white chocolate

CURRANT FILLING

8 ounces red currants, fresh or frozen

1 tablespoon cornstarch

CRUMBLE TOPPING

1. Mix the flour, sugar, baking powder, salt, and vanilla extract in a bowl. Add the butter and pinch it into the flour until the dough is crumbly.
2. Chop the chocolate relatively fine and mix it with the crumble dough.

PREPARING THE FILLING AND ASSEMBLING AND BAKING THE PIE

1. Preheat the oven to 400°F.
2. To make the filling, pour the currants into a bowl and mix in the cornstarch. Divide the currants evenly among the little pie pans (*Note:* Do not use a springform pan, as the liquid will leak out.) Crumble the topping evenly over the berries.
3. Bake the pies on the lower rack of the oven for 35 minutes or until the topping is golden brown and the filling is bubbly. Remove the pies from the oven and let them cool slightly. Serve them with Vanilla Ice Cream (page 137), if desired.

CRISPY PEAR CRUMBLE PIE

Pears are clearly an underrated fruit for pies, and people tend to use apples more often than pears. I must admit that pears are not my absolute favorite fruit to eat raw, but in a pie, that's a whole other story. In this pie, you'll get the best of two worlds, crispy crumble both under and over the fruit. How good is that?

1 pie, about 8 inches in diameter, 8–10 servings

CRUMBLE TOPPING

1¼ cups all-purpose flour

1¼ cups rolled oats

⅔ cup Turbinado or raw cane sugar

¾ teaspoon ground cinnamon

¼ teaspoon sea salt

14 tablespoons (6 ounces) butter, at room temperature

PEAR FILLING

2¼ pounds firm pears (I like to use a mix of Anjou and Bosc.)

2 tablespoons all-purpose flour

2 tablespoons (1 ounce) butter

⅓ cup granulated sugar

½ teaspoon ground cinnamon

2 tablespoons cognac or dark rum

TIP: If you don't have time to wait for the butter to reach room temperature, microwave it, a few seconds at a time, on full power.

CRUMBLE TOPPING

1. Mix the flour, oats, Turbinado sugar, cinnamon, and salt in a bowl.
2. Add the butter and pinch it into the flour mixture until the dough is crumbly.

PREPARING THE FILLING AND ASSEMBLING AND BAKING THE PIE

1. Preheat the oven to 400°F.
2. Press a little more than half of the crumble dough into a pie pan (use a spoon to help, as the dough can easily stick between your fingers). Blind-bake the shell on the middle rack of the oven for about 15 minutes (see page 24). Remove the pan from the oven and let the shell cool. While the shell bakes, prepare the filling.
3. To make the filling, peel, core, and slice the pears. Put the slices in a bowl and mix in the flour. Pour the pears into the blind-baked shell.
4. Melt the butter in a heavy-bottom saucepan over medium heat. When the butter has melted, add the granulated sugar and lower the heat a little. The sugar should melt completely and turn golden brown. Be careful, though, that it does not burn. Stir occasionally. Stir in the cinnamon and then add the cognac or rum a little at a time (be supercareful because it can splash out). The mixture will now look as if it were separating, but continue stirring it over the heat until the mixture blends together.
5. Drizzle half of the butter caramel over the pears. Then crumble the rest of the topping over the pears and drizzle the remaining caramel over the topping.
6. Bake the pie on the lower rack of the oven for 15 minutes. Reduce the temperature to 350°F and bake for another 40 to 45 minutes, until the topping is golden brown and the filling is bubbly. If the pie topping darkens too much, cover it with parchment paper or aluminum foil. Remove the pie from the oven and let it cool. Vanilla Ice Cream (page 137) makes a nice pairing, if desired.

GALETTE WITH STRAWBERRIES AND RHUBARB

Sweet strawberries together with tart rhubarb is a heavenly combination. The pie dough with cream cheese in it produces a softer dough than one made with only butter. If you think it seems too soft, put the dough in the freezer for 5 minutes before you roll it out.

1 large galette, 6–8 servings

PIECRUST

1¼ cups all-purpose flour

1 tablespoon granulated sugar

¼ teaspoon sea salt

5 tablespoons (2⅔ ounces) cold butter

3½ ounces cold cream cheese

1–2 tablespoons ice-cold water

STRAWBERRY AND RHUBARB FILLING

8 ounces fresh strawberries

8 ounces rhubarb (about 3 stalks)

6 tablespoons granulated sugar

Finely grated zest of 1 lemon

1 tablespoon freshly squeezed lemon juice

½ teaspoon ground cardamom

3 tablespoons cornstarch

GLAZE

1 egg

1 tablespoon milk

Pinch of sea salt

1½ teaspoons Turbinado or raw cane sugar

PIECRUST

1. Mix the flour, granulated sugar, and salt in a bowl. Dice the butter and add it to the flour mixture. Use your fingers to pinch in the butter until the dough is crumbly. Add the cream cheese and mix it in with a fork until the dough is again crumbly.
2. Add the cold water (begin with the smaller amount and gradually add more if the dough feels too dry) and mix it in with a fork. If you pick up a bit of the dough and it coheres when pressed together, it has enough water. Gently press the crumbles together for the dough. Wrap the dough in plastic wrap and refrigerate it for at least 1 hour, preferably overnight.

STRAWBERRY AND RHUBARB FILLING

1. Rinse and hull the strawberries, and cut them into halves or quarters (depending on how large the berries are).
2. Peel the rhubarb if it is coarse and cut it into ⅔-inch pieces.
3. Mix the strawberries and rhubarb in a bowl. Add the granulated sugar, grated lemon zest, lemon juice, cardamom, and cornstarch and gently stir them together.

ASSEMBLING AND BAKING THE PIE

1. Preheat the oven to 400°F.
2. On a lightly floured work surface, roll the dough out into a large circle, ⅛ inch thick. Carefully roll the dough onto the rolling pin and transfer it to a cutting board or baking sheet lined with parchment paper.
3. Pour the strawberries and rhubarb onto the dough circle, leaving 2½ to 2¾ inches around the edge free of filling. Fold the edge up around the berries, pressing down so the dough stays in place.
4. Put the galette in the freezer for about 15 minutes (so that it will hold its shape better in the oven when baking).
5. Take the galette out of the freezer and place it on a baking sheet lined with parchment paper.
6. To make the glaze, whisk the egg with the milk and salt. Brush the edges with the glaze and then sprinkle them with Turbinado sugar. Bake the galette on the lower rack of the oven for 40 to 45 minutes, until the pie is golden brown and the filling is bubbly and soft. Remove the galette from the oven and let it cool completely. Serve the galette with Whipped Honey Crème Fraîche (see page 141), if desired.

APPLE AND PEAR GALETTE

According to me, this apple and pear galette has the world's best pie-crust dough. I love hazelnuts, and this galette has loads of them, both in the dough and in the nut filling hidden under the fruit. If you prefer, it's perfectly fine to substitute orange juice for the cognac.

1 large galette, 6–8 servings

TOASTED HAZELNUTS

4 ounces hazelnuts

PIECRUST

1⅓ cups all-purpose flour

2 tablespoons granulated sugar

¼ teaspoon sea salt

2¼ ounces toasted hazelnuts (from the nuts above)

14 tablespoons (6 ounces) cold butter

2–4 tablespoons ice-cold water

HAZELNUT PASTE

1¾ ounces toasted hazelnuts (from the nuts above)

¼ cup Turbinado or raw cane sugar

¼ teaspoon ground cardamom

1 tablespoon water

APPLE AND PEAR FILLING

1 pound apples

1 pound pears

4 tablespoons (1¾ ounces) butter

6 tablespoons Turbinado or raw cane sugar

¼ teaspoon sea salt

1 teaspoon ground cinnamon

2 tablespoons freshly squeezed orange juice

Finely grated zest of ½ orange

2 tablespoons cognac

2 tablespoons all-purpose flour

GLAZE

1 egg

1 tablespoon milk

Pinch of sea salt

1 tablespoon Turbinado or raw cane sugar

TOASTED HAZELNUTS

1. Preheat the oven to 350°F.
2. Spread out the 4 ounces of hazelnuts on a baking sheet and toast them in the oven for 8 to 10 minutes or until the nuts begin to smell nutty and take on a little color under the skin.
3. Remove the hazelnuts from the oven and let them cool for a few minutes. Put the nuts on a kitchen towel and rub them with the towel to remove the skins (as best you can). Let the nuts cool.

PIECRUST

1. Mix the flour, granulated sugar, and salt in a bowl.
2. In a blender or food processor, pulse 2¼ ounces of the toasted hazelnuts to a relatively fine meal. (If you add a few tablespoons of the flour mixture when you process the nuts, it will help grind the nuts more finely.) Pour the nut meal into the bowl with the flour mixture.
3. Dice the butter and add it to the flour mixture. Use your fingers to pinch in the butter until the dough is crumbly.
4. Add the cold water (begin with the smaller amount and gradually add more if the dough feels too dry) and mix it in with a fork. If you pick up a bit of the dough and it coheres when pressed together, it has enough water.
5. Lay a piece of plastic wrap over the dough and flatten the dough slightly. Cover the dough completely with plastic wrap and refrigerate it for at least 1 hour, preferably overnight.

HAZELNUT PASTE

In a blender or food processor, pulse the remaining 1¾ ounces of toasted hazelnuts with the Turbinado sugar and cardamom until the nuts are ground but some larger bits remain. Pour the mixture into a bowl and mix in the water for a cohesive paste.

APPLE AND PEAR FILLING

1. Peel, core, and dice the apples and pears.
2. Melt the butter in a saucepan, then add the fruit, Turbinado sugar, salt, cinnamon, orange juice, orange zest, and cognac. Bring the mixture to a boil and simmer it for 2 to 3 minutes, until the fruit releases some juice. Mix in the flour, stir, and let the filling simmer for a few more minutes, until the mixture thickens. Remove the filling from the heat and let it cool completely.

»»*The recipe continues on page 75.*»»

Assembling and Baking the Pie

1. Preheat the oven to 400°F.

2. Bring the piecrust dough to room temperature. It might need an extra 5 to 10 minutes if it feels too hard. On a lightly floured work surface, roll out two-thirds of the dough into a large circle $\frac{1}{8}$ inch thick. Carefully roll the dough onto the rolling pin and transfer it to a cutting board or baking sheet lined with parchment paper.

3. Spread the hazelnut paste evenly over the dough to within $2\frac{1}{2}$ to $2\frac{3}{4}$ inches of the edge.

4. Roll out the rest of the dough and cut 8 strips, and also cut out any other decorative pieces you'd like.

5. Pour the apple and pear filling over the hazelnut paste. Weave the strips into a lattice (see page 16). Fold the edges up over the filling. The dough might be rather fragile, but it doesn't matter if it splits. Just carefully press it with your fingers to repair any splits.

6. Put the galette in the freezer for about 15 minutes (so that it will hold its shape better in the oven when baking).

7. Take the galette out of the freezer and slide it onto a baking sheet lined with parchment paper, if it's not already on one.

8. To make the glaze, whisk the egg with the milk and salt. Brush the edges and the lattice-top crust with the glaze and then sprinkle the pie with Turbinado sugar. Bake the galette on the lower rack of the oven for 40 to 45 minutes, until it is golden brown and the filling is bubbly and soft. Remove the galette from the oven and let it cool completely. Serve it with Vanilla Ice Cream (see page 137), if desired.

GALETTE WITH APRICOTS, BLACKBERRIES, AND THYME

Select apricots that are soft but still firm and fine—not mushy. You don't often see thyme in sweet baked goods, but it makes for a very good flavor combination in this pie.

1 large galette, 6–8 servings

PIECRUST

1¼ cups all-purpose flour
1 tablespoon granulated sugar
¼ teaspoon sea salt
12 tablespoons (5¼ ounces) cold butter
3–5 tablespoons ice-cold water

FRANGIPANE (ALMOND CREAM)

5¼ tablespoons (2⅔ ounces) butter, at room temperature
⅓ cup granulated sugar
1 egg
⅔ cup (2 ounces) almond flour

APRICOT AND BLACKBERRY FILLING

6 tablespoons slivered almonds
1 pound apricots (about 10)
8 ounces blackberries, fresh or frozen
1¼ tablespoons granulated sugar
1 tablespoon cornstarch
1–2 teaspoons chopped fresh thyme

GLAZE

1 egg
1 tablespoon milk
Pinch of sea salt
1 tablespoon Turbinado or raw cane sugar

PIECRUST

1. Mix the flour, granulated sugar, and salt in a bowl. Dice the butter and add it to the flour mixture. Use your fingers to pinch in the butter until the dough is crumbly.
2. Add the cold water (begin with the smaller amount and gradually add more if the dough feels too dry) and mix it in with a fork. If you pick up a bit of the dough and it coheres when pressed together, it has enough water.
3. Lay a piece of plastic wrap over the dough and flatten the dough slightly. Cover the dough completely with plastic wrap and refrigerate it for at least 1 hour, preferably overnight.

FRANGIPANE

Beat the butter and granulated sugar until creamy. Add the egg and almond flour and beat until smooth and creamy.

APRICOT AND BLACKBERRY FILLING

1. Toast the slivered almonds in a hot, dry frying pan until they are golden brown and smell good. Stir occasionally. Set the nuts aside to cool.
2. Remove the pits from the apricots, slice the fruit, and mix it with the blackberries in a bowl. Mix in the granulated sugar, cornstarch, and chopped thyme.

ASSEMBLING AND BAKING THE PIE

1. Preheat the oven to 400°F.
2. On a lightly floured work surface, roll out the dough to a large circle ⅛ inch thick. Carefully roll the dough onto the rolling pin and transfer it to a cutting board or baking sheet lined with parchment paper.
3. Spread the frangipane evenly over the dough, leaving 2½ to 2¾ inches around the edge free of cream. Layer the apricot and blackberry mixture and the toasted slivered almonds on top of the frangipane. Fold the edges of the dough over the filling, pressing down slightly so the crust stays in place.
4. Put the galette in the freezer for about 15 minutes (so that it will hold its shape better in the oven when baking).
5. Take the galette out of the freezer and place it on a baking sheet lined with parchment paper.
6. To make the glaze, whisk the egg with the milk and salt. Brush the crust edges with the glaze and sprinkle the Turbinado sugar over the galette. Bake it on the lower rack of the oven for 45 to 50 minutes, until the piecrust is golden brown and the filling is bubbly. Remove the galette from the oven and let it cool completely. Serve the galette with Vanilla Ice Cream (see page 137), if desired.

GLUTEN-FREE GALETTES WITH NECTARINES AND RASPBERRIES

Here's a delicate and delicious pie-crust made with rice flour and buckwheat flour. The recipe makes three smaller galettes, but, of course, one large pie will be just as good.

The dough is excellent for using in other recipes in this book, such as Pie Pops (page 92) or Hand Pies with Pears and Ginger (page 93). If you want to make a double-crust pie with the gluten-free dough, I recommend simply doubling the amounts in this recipe.

3 small galettes, 6 inches in diameter, 6–8 servings

GLUTEN-FREE PIECRUST
⅔ cup buckwheat flour
⅔ cup rice flour
1 tablespoon granulated sugar
¼ teaspoon sea salt
12 tablespoons (5¼ ounces) cold butter
3–4 tablespoons ice-cold water

NECTARINE AND RASPBERRY FILLING
3 tablespoons Turbinado or raw cane sugar
2 tablespoons cornstarch
¼ teaspoon sea salt
1½ pounds (23 ounces) nectarines (about 4)
4½ ounces raspberries, fresh or frozen
Finely grated zest and freshly squeezed juice of ½ lemon

GLAZE
1 egg
1 tablespoon milk
Pinch of sea salt
1 tablespoon Turbinado or raw cane sugar

GLUTEN-FREE PIECRUST
1. Mix the buckwheat and rice flours, granulated sugar, and salt in a bowl.
2. Dice the butter and add it to the flour mixture. Use your fingers to pinch in the butter until the dough is crumbly.
3. Add the cold water (begin with the smaller amount and gradually add more if the dough feels too dry) and mix it in with a fork. If you pick up a bit of the dough and it coheres when pressed together, it has enough water.
4. Lay a piece of plastic wrap over the dough and flatten it slightly. Cover the dough completely with plastic wrap and refrigerate it for at least 1 hour, but preferably overnight.

ASSEMBLING AND BAKING THE PIE
1. Preheat the oven to 400°F.
2. Remove the dough from the refrigerator and divide it into three equal pieces. On a well-floured work surface (rice flour works well), roll out each piece of dough to a circle ⅛ inch thick. The dough will be relatively fragile, so make sure there is enough flour on the work surface, lifting the dough to add more as you roll it out. By carefully rolling the dough circles onto the rolling pin one at a time, transfer each one to a cutting board or baking sheet lined with parchment paper.
3. To make the filling, mix the Turbinado sugar, cornstarch, and salt in a small bowl. Sprinkle a little of this sugar mixture over the dough circles, leaving 2½ to 2¾ inches all around the edge free of the mixture.
4. Remove the pits from the nectarines and slice the fruit. Divide the nectarines and raspberries among the pies. Sprinkle the rest of the sugar mixture on the fruit. Sprinkle the lemon zest over the fruit, then squeeze the lemon juice over it. Fold the edges of the dough up over the filling, pressing down slightly so the crust stays in place.
5. Put the galettes in the freezer for about 15 minutes (so that they will hold their shape better in the oven when baking).
6. Take the galettes out of the freezer and place them on a baking sheet lined with parchment paper.
7. To make the glaze, whisk the egg with the milk and salt. Brush the crust edges with the glaze and then sprinkle the dough with the Turbinado sugar. Bake the galettes on the lower rack of the oven for 20 minutes and then reduce the temperature to 350°F. Bake the galettes for another 20 to 25 minutes, until the edges are golden brown. Remove the galettes from the oven and let them cool completely. Serve with Vanilla Ice Cream (see page 137) on the side, if desired.

| MINIPIES AND TARTS |

RASPBERRY TURNOVERS

"Turnovers" is an amusing name for a pie, but they are called that because the filling is placed on the dough and the edges are turned over to the other side. Very forgiving, and no dough goes to waste.

6 turnovers

PIECRUST

6 squares of frozen puff pastry dough (9½ ounces) or 1 batch of Easy Flaky Pastry Dough (page 14)

RASPBERRY FILLING

5¼ ounces raspberries, fresh or frozen

3 tablespoons granulated sugar

1 tablespoon cornstarch

1 tablespoon freshly squeezed lemon juice

Finely grated zest of 1 lemon

⅓ cup ricotta cheese

1 tablespoon honey

GLAZE

1 egg

1 tablespoon milk

Pinch of sea salt

2 tablespoons slivered almonds

1 tablespoon Turbinado or raw cane sugar

RASPBERRY FILLING

1. Mix the raspberries with the granulated sugar in a saucepan. Bring the mixture to a boil.
2. In a small cup, dissolve the cornstarch in the lemon juice. Add the lemon zest. Stir the mixture into the raspberries. Let the mixture simmer for a few minutes, until it thickens somewhat. Remove the filling from the heat and let it cool completely.

ASSEMBLING AND BAKING THE TURNOVERS

1. Preheat the oven to 400°F.
2. Thaw the sheets of pastry dough on a baking sheet lined with parchment paper.
3. When the pastry has thawed but is still cold, divide the raspberry filling evenly among the squares, leaving about ½ to ¾ inch free of filling all around.
4. Mix the ricotta cheese with the honey and spoon it on the raspberries.
5. Brush the edges with water, then fold up the pasty to form a triangle, and press the edges together with a fork. Put the turnovers in the freezer for 10 minutes.
6. To make the glaze, whisk the egg with the milk and salt. Brush the turnovers with the glaze. Sprinkle the slivered almonds on top and then the Turbinado sugar. Use a knife to make a little slit in each pie.
7. Bake the turnovers on the middle rack of the oven for 20 to 25 minutes, until they have a good color. Remove the turnovers from the oven and let them cool completely.

FRIED APPLE PIES
WITH CARAMEL

These fantastically good fried pies are filled with apples and caramel. They are at their best when freshly fried, so eat them while they are still warm.

10 small pies

PIECRUST

1 cup + 2 tablespoons all-purpose flour
2 teaspoons granulated sugar
¼ teaspoon sea salt
½ teaspoon ground cinnamon
7 tablespoons (3½ ounces) cold butter
3–5 tablespoons ice-cold water

APPLE FILLING

8 ounces apples (about 2 apples)
3 tablespoons granulated sugar
2 tablespoons (1 ounce) butter
¼ teaspoon sea salt
½ teaspoon ground cinnamon
1 teaspoon cornstarch
1 teaspoon freshly squeezed lemon juice

FOR FRYING

3 cups vegetable oil (for example, corn oil)

TIP: For a crisper crust (think of the apple pies at those fast food hamburger chains), you can both bake and fry the pies.
1. Preheat the oven to 400°F.
2. Place the pies on a baking sheet lined with parchment paper. Brush the pies with beaten egg, then cut a few slits in each pie and sprinkle them with sugar. Bake the pies on the middle rack of the oven for 20 minutes. Remove the pies from the oven and cool them slightly.
3. Heat the oil to 350°F and fry the pies for 2 to 3 minutes.

PIECRUST

1. Mix the flour, sugar, salt, and cinnamon in a bowl. Dice the butter and add it to the flour mixture. Pinch in the butter until the dough is crumbly.
2. Add the water gradually and mix it in with a fork. If the dough coheres when pressed together, it has enough water.
3. Lay a piece of plastic wrap over the dough and flatten the dough slightly. Cover the dough completely with plastic wrap and refrigerate it for at least 1 hour, preferably overnight.

APPLE FILLING

1. Peel, core, and cut the apples into ⅜ x ⅜-inch dice.
2. Pour the sugar into a heavy-bottom saucepan and heat it over medium heat. When the sugar begins to melt around the edges, carefully stir it in toward the center until all the sugar has melted and begins to turn golden brown—make sure it doesn't burn.
3. Carefully add the butter, a little at a time, to the melted sugar, stirring after each addition of butter.
4. Stir in the apple pieces, salt, and cinnamon and let the mixture simmer for 4 to 5 minutes, until the apples have softened.
5. In a small cup, dissolve the cornstarch in the lemon juice and then pour it into the apple mixture, stirring as you pour. Continuing to stir, let the filling simmer for about 1 minute, until it thickens slightly. Remove from the heat and let cool completely.

BAKING AND FRYING

1. Remove the piecrust dough from the refrigerator; leave it at room temperature for a few minutes if it feels too hard to roll out right away. Roll out the dough on a floured work surface. Cut out small circles, about 3 inches in diameter, using a cookie cutter, drinking glass, or small lid. Place half of the circles on a baking sheet lined with parchment paper.
2. Spoon 1 heaping tablespoon of filling onto each circle of dough on the baking sheet. Brush the edges with a little water, top the pie with another dough circle, and press them together. Make a pattern all around the edges with a fork. Place the pies in the refrigerator while you heat the oil.
3. Pour the oil into a heavy-bottom saucepan with high sides. The oil should be about 1¼ inches deep. Heat it to 350°F (check with a baking thermometer).
4. Fry the pies, two at a time, for 5 to 6 minutes, turning them after half of the frying time. Make sure the heat stays at about 350°F. Transfer the pies to paper towels with a slotted spoon. Let them cool slightly; serve with Vanilla Ice Cream (page 137), if desired.

PIE POPS

These pie pops are a little fiddly but make fun minipies. Challenge yourself with new decorations and a braided top crust. Make sure you use sticks that don't have any plastic. If you can't find good sticks made of paper, use wooden ice cream sticks. Or, of course, you can make the pies without sticks.

About 20 minipies

PIECRUST
1 cup all-purpose flour
1 tablespoon granulated sugar
¼ teaspoon sea salt
9 tablespoons (4½ ounces) cold butter
2–3 tablespoons ice-cold water

FILLINGS
Each of the filling amounts below is enough for 1 batch of piecrust dough.

BANOFFEE
1–2 bananas
6 tablespoons dulce de leche

NUTELLA AND CREAM CHEESE
6 tablespoons Nutella
¼ cup cream cheese

PEANUT BUTTER AND CHOCOLATE
1 ounce dark chocolate
6 tablespoons peanut butter

GLAZE
1 egg
1 tablespoon milk
Pinch of sea salt
1 tablespoon Turbinado or raw cane sugar

PIECRUST
1. Mix the flour, granulated sugar, and salt in a bowl. Dice the butter and add it to the flour mixture. Use your fingers to pinch in the butter until the dough is crumbly.
2. Add the water gradually and mix it in with a fork. If you pick up a bit of the dough and it coheres when pressed together, it has enough water.
3. Lay a piece of plastic wrap over the dough, flatten the dough somewhat, and then cover the dough completely with plastic wrap. Refrigerate the dough for at least 1 hour, preferably overnight.

ASSEMBLING THE PIES
1. Preheat the oven to 400°F.
2. Roll out the dough on a floured work surface. Cut out small circles, about 2¼ inches in diameter, using a cookie cutter, drinking glass, or lid. Place half of the circles on a piece of parchment paper.

WITH BANOFFEE FILLING
1. Slice the bananas thinly crosswise. Spoon 1 teaspoon of dulce de leche onto each dough circle and press in a banana slice.
2. Brush a little water all around the edge outside the filling and push a paper stick into the filling. Lay another dough circle on top and press the edges together. Freeze for 5 minutes and then transfer the pies and parchment paper to a baking sheet.

WITH NUTELLA AND CREAM CHEESE FILLING
1. Mix the Nutella and cream cheese in a bowl. Spoon ½ tablespoon of the filling onto each circle.
2. Brush a little water all around the edge outside the filling and push a paper stick into the filling. Place another dough circle on top and press the edges together. Freeze for 5 minutes and then transfer the pies and parchment paper to a baking sheet.

WITH PEANUT BUTTER AND CHOCOLATE FILLING
1. Chop the chocolate. Spoon 1 teaspoon of peanut butter onto each dough circle and press in a little chocolate.
2. Brush a little water all around the edge outside the filling and push a paper stick into the filling. Place another dough circle on top and press the edges together. Freeze for 5 minutes and then transfer the pies and parchment paper to a baking sheet.

GLAZING AND BAKING
1. To make the glaze, whisk the egg with the milk and salt. Brush the pies with the glaze and sprinkle them with the Turbinado sugar. If your pies don't have some air holes, cut a couple of slits.
2. Bake on the middle rack of the oven for 16 to 18 minutes, until the pies have begun to brown. Remove and let them cool completely.

HAND PIES WITH PEARS AND GINGER

Lovely small pies are perfect for eating with your hands. This recipe comes from the time when I was in Croatia and had a sudden urge to bake a pie. I had ginger and almonds, a large bag of pears from the fruit market, and the ingredients for pie dough. I didn't have any pie pans on hand, so I decided to make small pear pies with the ginger and homemade almond paste. Select firm pears that are not overripe for these small pies.

18–20 small pies

PIECRUST

1¼ cups all-purpose flour
1 tablespoon granulated sugar
¼ teaspoon sea salt
¼ teaspoon ground ginger
12 tablespoons (5¼ ounces) cold butter
3–5 tablespoons ice-cold water

ALMOND PASTE

1¾ ounces sweet almonds
2 tablespoons Turbinado or raw cane sugar
1–2 tablespoons water

PEAR FILLING

3 pears
2 tablespoons (1 ounce) butter
¼ cup Turbinado or raw cane sugar
¼ teaspoon ground cinnamon
½ teaspoon ground ginger
½ teaspoon vanilla extract
1 tablespoon freshly squeezed lemon or
    orange juice
¼ teaspoon sea salt
1 tablespoon all-purpose flour

GLAZE

1 egg
1 tablespoon milk
Pinch of sea salt
1–2 tablespoons Turbinado or raw cane sugar

PIECRUST

1. Mix the flour, granulated sugar, salt, and ginger in a bowl. Dice the butter and add it to the flour mixture. Use your fingers to pinch the butter into the flour until the dough is crumbly.
2. Add the water (begin with the smaller amount and gradually add more if the dough feels too dry) and mix it in with a fork. If you pick up a bit of the dough and it coheres when pressed together, it has enough water.
3. Lay a piece of plastic wrap over the dough, flatten the dough somewhat, and then cover the dough completely with plastic wrap. Refrigerate the dough for at least 1 hour, preferably overnight.

ALMOND PASTE

In a food processor, pulse the almonds and Turbinado sugar until the almonds are ground but still have a few larger bits left. Pour the almond mix into a bowl and stir in the water until the mixture is a paste.

PEAR FILLING

1. Peel, core, and cut the pears to about ⅜ x ⅜-inch dice.
2. Melt the butter in a saucepan. Add the pears along with the Turbinado sugar, cinnamon, ginger, vanilla extract, citrus juice, and salt. Bring the mixture to a boil and then simmer it for about 1 minute, until the fruit releases its juice. Stir in the flour and let the mixture simmer for another minute, until the filling thickens. Remove it from the heat and let it cool completely.

ASSEMBLING AND BAKING THE PIES

1. Preheat the oven to 400°F.
2. Roll out the dough on a floured work surface. Cut out small circles, about 3½ inches in diameter, using a cookie cutter, drinking glass, or lid. Place the dough circles on a baking sheet or cutting board lined with parchment paper.
3. Spread a bit of almond paste in the center of each dough circle and spoon 2 tablespoons of pear filling on top. Brush the edges with a little water and fold the pies into half-moon shapes. Make a pattern around the edges with a fork. Put the pies in the freezer for 10 minutes.
4. Transfer the pies with the parchment paper to a baking sheet.
5. To make the glaze, whisk the egg with the milk and salt. Brush the pies with the egg mixture and then sprinkle them with the Turbinado sugar. Cut 2 or 3 slits in each pie. Bake the pies on the middle rack of the oven for 25 to 30 minutes, until the pies are goldern brown. Remove the pies from the oven and let them cool completely.

FLAKY PASTRY TARTS WITH NO-COOK BLUEBERRY JAM AND WHIPPED CREAM

The easiest pie you can make uses prepared flaky puff pastry that is topped with berry jam. Assemble these tarts immediately before serving, so the pastry base won't get soggy.

8 servings

FLAKY PASTRY BASE

1 batch Easy Flaky Pastry Dough (page 14), or 4 rectangles frozen puff pastry (about 14 ounces)

1 egg

1 tablespoon milk

¼ teaspoon sea salt

BLUEBERRY JAM

5¼ ounces (1 cup) blueberries, fresh or frozen

2 tablespoons honey

WHIPPED YOGURT

¼ cup slivered almonds

1 cup whipping cream

6 tablespoons Turkish or Greek yogurt (10% fat)

2 tablespoons honey

2 tablespoons confectioners' sugar

FLAKY PASTRY BASE

1. Preheat the oven to 400°F.
2. Roll out the pastry dough into a rectangle, about 4¾ x 11 inches, and divide it into eight pieces. Lay the pieces on a baking sheet lined with parchment paper. (If you use frozen puff pastry, let it thaw on the parchment paper for 15 to 20 minutes. Then divide each pastry rectangle in half so you have eight pieces.)
3. Score around each rectangle with a knife, about ⅜ inch in from the outer edge, but do not cut all the way through the sheet. Prick the center with a fork.
4. Whisk the egg, milk, and salt in a small bowl. Brush the edges of the pastry pieces with this mixture.
5. Bake the rectangles on the middle rack of the oven for 20 to 22 minutes, until the pastry puffs up and is golden brown. Remove the pastries from the oven and let them cool to room temperature.

BLUEBERRY JAM AND WHIPPED YOGURT

1. Mix the blueberries and honey in a bowl.
2. Toast the slivered almonds in a hot, dry frying pan until they are golden brown and smell good. Stir occasionally. Let them cool.
3. Whip the cream until it begins to thicken, and then whisk in the yogurt and honey. Stir in a couple of tablespoons of the liquid from the blueberry mixture so the cream will have a pretty color.
4. Spoon the cream onto the pastry shells. Top it with the blueberries and toasted almonds. Sift the confectioners' sugar over the tarts.

EASY TART WITH FRESH BERRIES

This easy tart is really one of the simplest pie recipes you can make, and it's a perfect way to use up the wonderful fresh berries of summer.

About 9 servings

PIECRUST

1 cup + 2 tablespoons all-purpose flour
6 tablespoons (1½ ounces) almond flour
1 tablespoon granulated sugar
¼ teaspoon sea salt
12 tablespoons (5¼ ounces) cold butter
2–4 tablespoons ice-cold water

GLAZE

1 egg
1 tablespoon milk
Pinch of sea salt

MASCARPONE AND BERRY TOPPING

8 ounces mascarpone
2 tablespoons granulated sugar
½ teaspoon vanilla extract
14 ounces mixed berries or fruit
A little fresh mint or lemon balm
1 tablespoon confectioners' sugar

PIECRUST

1. Mix the all-purpose flour, almond flour, granulated sugar, and salt in a bowl. Dice the butter and add it to the flour mixture. Use your fingers to pinch in the butter until the dough is crumbly.
2. Add the cold water (begin with the smaller amount and gradually add more if the dough feels too dry) and mix it in with a fork. If you pick up a bit of the dough and it coheres when pressed together, it has enough water.
3. Lay a piece of plastic wrap over the dough, flatten the dough somewhat, and then cover the dough completely with plastic wrap. Refrigerate the dough for at least 1 hour, preferably overnight.

ASSEMBLING AND BAKING THE TART

1. Preheat the oven to 400°F. On a floured work surface, roll out the dough to a rectangle about ¼ inch thick. Transfer the dough to a baking sheet lined with parchment paper.
2. To make the glaze, whisk the egg, milk, and salt in a small bowl. Brush the tart base with the egg mixture and bake it on the middle rack of the oven for 20 to 25 minutes, until the pastry is golden brown.
3. Remove the tart from the oven and let it cool completely.

MASCARPONE AND BERRY TOPPING

1. Whisk the mascarpone together with the granulated sugar and vanilla extract. Spread the mascarpone cream on top of the tart base.
2. Sprinkle the berries evenly over the pastry, garnish them with mint or lemon balm, and sift confectioners' sugar on top. Cut the tart into pieces and serve immediately.

BANANA TARTE TATIN

When you make this pie, it is important to use a frying pan or something similar that will tolerate the heat of both the stovetop and the oven. A cast iron pan is ideal, but not one with a wood or plastic handle. Also be very careful when you turn out the pie, because the sauce will be extremely hot. Cover your arms to be on the safe side.

**1 pie, 7 inches in diameter,
6–8 servings**

PIECRUST
1 batch Easy Flaky Pastry Dough (page 14) or ready-made puff pastry, 8–10½ ounces

BANANA FILLING
2 tablespoons (1 ounce) butter
⅓ cup granulated sugar
¼ teaspoon sea salt
¼ teaspoon ground cinnamon
3 small bananas

PIECRUST
1. Take the pastry dough out of the refrigerator and leave it at room temperature for a few minutes if it feels hard. On a lightly floured work surface, roll out the dough into a circle that is a little larger than the pan you will use (1¼ to 1½ inches larger in diameter). Lay the dough circle on a plate lined with parchment paper and refrigerate it while you prepare the rest of the tart.
2. Preheat the oven to 400°F.

PREPARE THE FILLING AND BAKE
1. Melt the butter in a frying pan over medium heat. Add the sugar and salt and reduce the temperature slightly. The sugar should melt completely and become golden brown. Stir it occasionally and be careful that it doesn't burn. Stir in the cinnamon and remove the pan from the heat.
2. Slice the bananas down the center and arrange them in the melted sugar in the frying pan. Be careful not to burn yourself.
3. Lay the rolled-out flaky pastry dough over the bananas. Now you have to work as quickly as possible. Use a wooden spoon to poke the edges of the dough down around the bananas. Use a knife to cut a few holes.
4. Place the pan on the middle rack of the oven and bake the pie for about 25 minutes, until the pastry is golden brown. (*Note:* Don't forget that the pan is hot when you take it out—use thick pot holders.)
5. Let the pie cool for a couple of minutes. Take out a plate that is somewhat larger than the pan. Place the plate over the pan and flip both the pan and the plate so the pie falls out onto the plate. Be careful!
6. Let the pie cool for about 20 minutes and serve it with Vanilla Ice Cream (page 137), if desired.

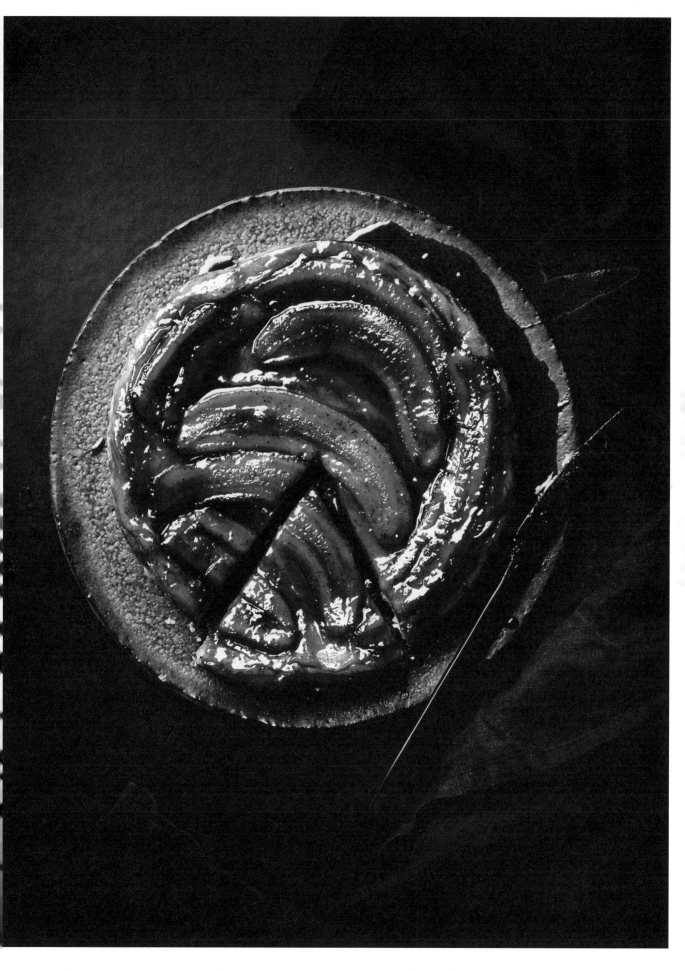

FIG TART WITH MASCARPONE, ROSEMARY, AND WALNUTS

This tart is a little like a pizza, but also not. To begin with, it's sweet. You can substitute other fruits for the figs. For example, why not try sliced peaches, plums, or apricots?

1 large pizza tart, 6–8 servings

PIECRUST

1 cup all-purpose flour
2 teaspoons baking powder
2 teaspoons granulated sugar
¼ teaspoon sea salt
9 tablespoons (4½ ounces) cold butter
2–4 tablespoons ice-cold water

HONEY-ROASTED NUTS

¾ cup (3½ ounces) walnuts
1 tablespoon (½ ounce) butter
2 tablespoons granulated sugar
1 tablespoon honey
¼ teaspoon salt
¼ teaspoon ground cinnamon
A few sprigs fresh rosemary

HONEY MASCARPONE

8 ounces mascarpone
3 tablespoons honey
½ teaspoon vanilla extract

FIG TOPPING

5–6 fresh figs
A few sprigs fresh rosemary (optional)
2 tablespoons honey (optional)

PIECRUST

1. Mix the flour, baking powder, sugar, and salt in a bowl. Dice the butter and add it to the flour mixture. Use your fingers to pinch in the butter until the dough is crumbly.
2. Add the water (begin with the smaller amount and gradually add more if the dough feels too dry) and mix it in with a fork. If you pick up a bit of the dough and it coheres when pressed together, it has enough water.
3. Lay a piece of plastic wrap over the dough, flatten the dough somewhat, and then cover the dough completely with plastic wrap. Refrigerate it for at least 30 minutes.

HONEY-ROASTED NUTS

1. Put the walnuts, butter, sugar, honey, and salt in a frying pan (preferably a nonstick pan).
2. Stirring regularly, melt the mixture over medium heat. Add the cinnamon and chopped rosemary. Let the mixture bubble over low heat for 7 to 10 minutes, until the nuts begin to color and the liquid is golden brown. Stir occasionally.
3. Spread the nuts out on a piece of parchment paper. Let them cool and then chop them into smaller pieces.

HONEY MASCARPONE

Mix the mascarpone, honey, and vanilla extract in a bowl.

ASSEMBLING AND BAKING THE TART

1. Preheat the oven to 400°F.
2. Slice the figs.
3. On a floured work surface, roll out the dough until it is about ¼ inch thick. Transfer it to a baking sheet lined with parchment paper.
4. Spread about two-thirds of the mascarpone cream over the pastry. Arrange the figs on the cream and then dollop the rest of the cream on top. If you like, add a few sprigs of rosemary. Bake the tart on the middle rack of the oven for 20 to 23 minutes, until the pastry and mascarpone begin to have a little color. Remove the tart from the oven and let it cool. Sprinkle the roasted nuts over the tart. Optional: Garnish the tart with some rosemary and a little extra honey drizzled over the top.

| SINGLE-CRUST PIES |

CRÈME BRÛLÉE PIE WITH VANILLA AND CITRUS

One of my favorite desserts is crème brûlée. I also love citrus fruits, so this crème brûlée pie is perfect for me. If you don't want a citrus flavor but would prefer just a pure crème brûlée pie, you can omit the orange peel in the cream and use milk instead of the citrus juice.

1 pie, 8 x 13¾ inches, 6–8 servings

PIECRUST

1 cup all-purpose flour
2 tablespoons granulated sugar
¼ teaspoon salt
7 tablespoons (3½ ounces) butter

FILLING

1 vanilla bean
3 tablespoons granulated sugar
1¼ cups whipping cream
1 teaspoon finely grated blood orange zest
    (1–2 blood oranges)
6 tablespoons freshly pressed juice from
    blood orange and grapefruit
4 egg yolks

2 tablespoons Turbinado or raw cane sugar
2 blood oranges
1 grapefruit

TIP: The pie can be prepared ahead of time (through step 3 of the filling), the day before you serve it. Loosely cover the pie and refrigerate it. If there is excess moisture on the surface, I recommend carefully laying a piece of paper towel over the top to absorb the moisture before caramelizing the top with the brûlée torch immediately before serving.

PIECRUST

1. Preheat the oven to 350°F.
2. Mix the flour, granulated sugar, and salt in a bowl. Melt the butter and blend it with the dry ingredients by pinching it into the flour until the dough coheres.
3. Press the dough into an oblong pan and prick the bottom and sides of the dough with a fork. Bake the dough on the middle rack of the oven for 21 to 23 minutes, until the crust begins to take on color. Remove the pie shell from the oven and let it cool.
4. Reduce the oven temperature to 300°F.

FILLING

1. Split the vanilla bean lengthwise, scrape out the seeds, and put them in a saucepan along with the bean pod. Mix in 1½ tablespoons of the granulated sugar, the whipping cream, and the grated orange zest. Stir the mixture and heat it until it is steaming hot. Remove the pan from the heat. Add the citrus juice and place a lid on the pan. Let the mixture stand for 10 minutes.
2. Whisk the egg yolks with 1½ tablespoons of the granulated sugar in a bowl. Blend this with the cream mixture. Let it cool.
3. Strain the mixture and pour it into a pitcher (the filling is very loose). Place the blind-baked pie shell on the middle rack of the oven. Carefully pour the filling into the shell. Bake the pie until the filling is firm around the edges but still a little wobbly in the center, 34 to 36 minutes. Remove the pie from the oven, let it cool to room temperature, and then refrigerate it for at least 2 hours.
4. Sprinkle 1 tablespoon of the Turbinado sugar in an even layer over the tart and caramelize it with a brûlée torch.
5. Cut thin slices of the oranges and grapefruit and then cut away the peel. Arrange the slices on top of the tart and sprinkle the remaining 1 tablespoon of Turbinado sugar over the fruit slices and the tart. Caramelize the surface again with the brûlée torch. Serve the tart immediately.

LIME PIE WITH COCONUT AND WHITE CHOCOLATE

Lime pie always reminds me of the time when I started my blog many years ago. It was one of my very first Blogposts. I don't think that I shared my recipe then, and so it's time to do it now. This version perfectly combines white chocolate and coconut with the tart lime juice.

1 pie, 8 inches in diameter, 6–8 servings

PIECRUST

5¼ tablespoons (2⅔ ounces) butter
6 ounces digestive biscuits or graham
 crackers
¼ cup coconut flakes
1¾ ounces white chocolate

LIME FILLING

1 can (14 ounces) sweetened condensed
 milk
4 egg yolks
Grated zest and juice of 4 limes (about 6
 tablespoons juice)
6 tablespoons Turkish or Greek yogurt
 (10% fat)

TOPPING

1 cup whipping cream
5 tablespoons Turkish or Greek yogurt
 (10% fat)
1 ounce (about 2 tablespoons) white
 chocolate
Grated zest of ½ lime
A few lime slices

TIP: If you want to use the egg whites, this pie can be topped with a meringue. See the Citrus Meringue Pie (page 110) for the instructions.

PIE SHELL

1. Preheat the oven to 350°F.
2. Melt the butter and let it cool.
3. In a food processor, pulse the digestive biscuits, coconut flakes, and white chocolate to fine crumbs. Mix in the melted butter and press the mixture into a pan with a removable bottom.
4. Blind-bake the shell (see page 24) on the middle rack of the oven for 12 to 14 minutes or until the shell begins to color. Remove the pie shell from the oven and let it cool for at least 15 minutes.

LIME FILLING

1. In a bowl, beat the sweetened condensed milk with the egg yolks, the lime zest and juice, and the yogurt until the mixture is smooth. Pour the filling into the pie shell and bake the pie on the middle rack of the oven for 15 to 17 minutes, or until the filling is firm but still a little wobbly in the center.
2. Remove the pie from the oven and let it cool completely before refrigerating it for at least 2 hours.

TOPPING

Whip the cream with the yogurt until it thickens. Use an ice-cream scoop to mound the cream on the pie. Top the cream with a little slivered white chocolate, grated lime zest, and if you like, a few thin slices of lime.

CITRUS MERINGUE PIE

Through the years, I've tested many variations of citrus and meringue pies, and this is my absolute favorite. This version is creamy and sweet but still just tart enough. I like using more than one kind of citrus fruit when I make these pies, but it works just as well with only one kind, such as lemon or orange. You'll need a brûlée torch for this recipe.

3 small pies, 5¼ inches in diameter, 6–8 servings

PIECRUST

1⅓ cups all-purpose flour
¼ cup confectioners' sugar
¼ teaspoon sea salt
9 tablespoons (4½ ounces) butter

CITRUS FILLING

1 can (14 ounces) sweetened condensed milk
3 egg yolks (save the whites for the meringue topping)
⅓ cup freshly squeezed citrus juice (I used a combination of lemon, orange, and clementine orange juice)
2 teaspoons finely grated citrus zest (I used half orange, half lemon peel)
¼ teaspoon sea salt

MERINGUE TOPPING

3 egg whites
¾ cup granulated sugar

PIE SHELL

1. Preheat the oven to 350°F.
2. Mix the flour, confectioners' sugar, and salt in a bowl. Melt the butter and stir it into the flour mixture. Pinch in the butter with your fingers until the dough coheres. Divide the dough into the three pie pans. Press it out to fill each pan and then prick the bottom and sides with a fork. Blind-bake the shells (see page 24) on the lower rack of the oven for 18 minutes or until the bottom of the shell begins to color. Remove the piecrust from the oven and let it cool.

CITRUS FILLING AND MERINGUE TOPPING

1. In a bowl, beat the sweetened condensed milk with the egg yolks, citrus juice, citrus zest, and salt until smooth. Pour the filling equally into the pie shells and bake them on the middle rack of the oven for 15 to 17 minutes or until the filling is firm but still a little wobbly in the center. Remove the pies from the oven and let them cool.
2. For the meringue topping, pour the egg whites and granulated sugar into a heatproof bowl and place it over a simmering water bath. Beat the mixture with a hand whisk until it reaches 150°F or the sugar melts (carefully rub a little of the mixture between your fingers to determine whether the sugar is smooth or still granular) and the mixture is hot.
3. Remove the bowl from the water bath and use an electric mixer to beat the meringue until it is quite thick and has cooled. Pipe the meringue over the citrus filling and caramelize it with a brûlée torch.

RED CURRANT PIE WITH MERINGUE TOPPING

This red currant pie is fresh and tart, with an extravagant layer of meringue that is crispy on the outside and soft inside. The base is tender and tasty and reminiscent of Swedish caramel cookies. Don't forget to butter the pan with a little melted butter before you add the pie dough because otherwise the crust will stick to the pan.

1 pie, 7 inches in diameter, 6–8 servings

PIECRUST
¾ cup all-purpose flour

½ teaspoon baking powder

¼ cup granulated sugar

5¼ tablespoons (2⅔ ounces) butter, at room temperature

Finely grated zest of 1 small lemon

1 egg yolk (save the egg white for the meringue topping)

RED CURRANT FILLING
8 ounces red currants, fresh or frozen, stems removed

1½ tablespoons granulated sugar

1 tablespoon cornstarch

1 tablespoon water

MERINGUE TOPPING
3 egg whites, plus the 1 egg white saved above

¾ cup granulated sugar

4 teaspoons cornstarch

PIECRUST
1. Preheat the oven to 350°F.
2. Mix the flour, baking powder, and sugar in a bowl. Add the butter and lemon zest to the flour mixture. Pinch in the butter with your fingers until the dough coheres. Whisk the egg yolk, add it to the dough, and blend it in quickly. Press the dough into a buttered springform pan and refrigerate it for 15 minutes.
3. Bake the shell on the middle rack of the oven for 23 to 25 minutes or until the shell begins to take on color. Remove the piecrust from the oven and let it cool.

CURRANT FILLING
Mix the currants in a saucepan with the sugar. Bring the mixture to a boil. In a small cup, dissolve the cornstarch in the water and then stir it into the saucepan with the currants. Let the filling simmer for a minute or so, until the mixture thickens. Remove the filling from the heat and let it cool.

MERINGUE TOPPING
1. Pour the egg whites into a bowl. Beat them until they are foamy and then add the sugar, a small amount at a time, as you continue beating. Beat the mixture until the meringue is very thick and shiny. Beat in the cornstarch at the end.
2. Pour the currant filling into the pie shell. Spread the meringue on top (but not all the way to the edge because it will spread as it bakes). Bake the pie on the lower rack of the oven for 20 to 23 minutes, until the meringue is golden brown. Remove the pie from the oven and let it cool completely.

BANANA CREAM PIE

This banana cream pie has a sweet-salty, crispy base with peanuts, vanilla cream, bananas, whipping cream, and caramel sauce—there isn't much that beats this combination. The pie should be eaten the same day it is baked or the crust will get soggy.

1 pie, about 8 inches in diameter, 8–10 servings

PIECRUST

1 cup all-purpose flour
1 tablespoon granulated sugar
About 1 ounce, or ¼ cup, salted peanuts
9 tablespoons (4½ ounces) cold butter
1 egg yolk (save the white for brushing the baked pie shell)
2–4 tablespoons ice-cold water

VANILLA CREAM

2¼ cups whole milk
1 teaspoon vanilla extract
¼ teaspoon ground cinnamon
6 tablespoons granulated sugar
⅓ cup cornstarch
5 egg yolks
4 tablespoons (1¾ ounces) butter

TOPPING

Caramel Sauce with Rum (page 139)
3–4 bananas
1¼ cups whipping cream
1 teaspoon ground cinnamon

TIP: To prevent the pie base from getting soggy from the filling, try brushing the blind-baked pie shell with a little melted chocolate (any kind) and let it set. This will make the pie last a little longer, and will also be delicious.

PIECRUST

1. Mix the flour and sugar in a bowl. In a food processor, pulse the peanuts to a relatively fine meal and then mix them with the flour and sugar. Dice the butter and add it to the flour mixture. Pinch the butter in with your fingers until the dough coheres. Whisk the egg yolk, add it to the dough, and blend it in quickly.
2. Add the water gradually (adding more if the dough feels too dry) and mix it in with a fork. If you pick up a bit of the dough and it coheres when pressed together, it has enough liquid.
3. Lay a piece of plastic wrap over the dough, flatten the dough somewhat, and then cover the dough completely with plastic wrap. Refrigerate the pie shell for at least 1 hour, preferably overnight.

VANILLA CREAM

1. Pour the milk into a saucepan and bring it to a boil. Stir occasionally.
2. Mix the vanilla extract, cinnamon, sugar, cornstarch, and egg yolks in a bowl and then beat this mixture into a thick cream.
3. Pour about 6 tablespoons of the warm milk into the egg mixture and stir it well. Pour the entire mixture back into the saucepan and heat it on medium, stirring constantly until the mixture thickens well. Remove the pan from the heat and let it cool for a few minutes.
4. Add the butter and stir until it melts. Pour the cream into a bowl and cover it with plastic wrap placed directly on the surface of the cream (this prevents a skin from forming). Let the filling cool at room temperature and then refrigerate it until it is completely cold. You can speed up the cooling process by placing the bowl over an ice-cold water bath and stirring occasionally before covering and refrigerating.

ASSEMBLING AND BAKING THE PIE

1. Preheat the oven to 400°F.
2. Prepare the Caramel Sauce with Rum.
3. On a floured work surface, roll out the dough until it is ⅛ inch thick. Lay the dough in the pie pan and crimp the edge (see page 18). Freeze for 10 minutes.
4. Cut out a square of parchment paper a little larger than the bottom diameter of the pie pan. Place the paper in the pie shell. Fill the shell with dried beans or uncooked rice.
5. Blind-bake the shell (see page 24) on the middle rack of the oven for 15 to 17 minutes or until the edges begin to color. Remove from the oven and remove the paper with the beans or rice. Brush the shell bottom with the reserved egg white, and bake the crust for another 15 to 20 minutes. Remove and let cool.
6. Layer the vanilla cream and thin slices of banana in the shell, ending with a layer of vanilla cream.
7. To top, whip the cream and spread it on the vanilla cream filling. Sift the cinnamon over it and drizzle with caramel sauce.

COCONUT CREAM PIE

Here's a pie for everyone who loves coconut. If you can't find toasted coconut chips, it's easy to toast coconut flakes in a hot, dry frying pan.

1 pie, about 8 inches in diameter, 8–10 servings

PIE SHELL

1½ cups rolled oats

¾ cup grated coconut

¼ cup light Muscovado sugar (hard packed into measuring cup)

¼ teaspoon sea salt

7 tablespoons (3½ ounces) butter

COCONUT FILLING

½ cup whole milk

1¾ cups coconut milk

½ teaspoon vanilla extract

6 tablespoons granulated sugar

3 egg yolks

4 tablespoons cornstarch

2 tablespoons (1 ounce) butter

1¼ cups grated coconut

TOPPING

1¼ cups whipping cream

6 tablespoons coconut chips (toasted coconut flakes)

PIE SHELL

1. Preheat the oven to 350°F.
2. In a food processor, pulse the oats and coconut to a fine meal. Add the Muscovado sugar and the salt and pulse the mixture a little more.
3. Melt the butter and blend it in with the oat mixture to form the dough. Press the dough into a springform pan. Bake the pie shell on the middle rack of the oven for 21 to 23 minutes, until it is golden brown. Remove the pie shell from the oven and let it cool completely.

COCONUT FILLING

1. Mix 6 tablespoons of the milk with the coconut milk, vanilla extract, and granulated sugar in a saucepan. Bring the mixture to a boil and then remove the saucepan from the heat.
2. Lightly whisk the egg yolks in a bowl. Pour a little of the warm milk mixture over the egg yolks, stirring constantly. Pour and whisk the egg mixture into the milk mixture in the saucepan.
3. In a small cup, dissolve the cornstarch with the remaining 2 tablespoons of milk. Put the saucepan with the milk-egg mixture back over the heat and pour and whisk in the cornstarch mixture. Let the mixture simmer for a couple of minutes as you whisk, until it has thickened well. Remove the saucepan from the heat and add the butter. Stir until the butter has melted. Stir in the coconut.
4. Place the saucepan over a cold-water bath and stir occasionally, until the coconut cream is cool. Pour the cream into the pie shell and refrigerate it until it is firm, about 3 to 4 hours.

TOPPING

Beat the whipping cream until it is firm. Pipe the whipped cream over the pie and then sprinkle coconut chips on top.

S'MORES PIE

This pie is my variation of s'mores; no wood fire needed to make it. For just one layer, you can make the chocolate filling by blending all the chocolate in a bowl and then mixing the hot cream into it, but I think it is nice in two layers. You'll need a brûlée torch for this recipe.

1 pie, about 8 inches in diameter, 8–10 servings

PIE SHELL
8 ounces graham crackers
7 tablespoons (3½ ounces) butter

CHOCOLATE FILLING
5¼ ounces milk chocolate
5¼ ounces dark chocolate (70% cacao)
1 cup whipping cream

MERINGUE TOPPING
4 large egg whites
1 cup granulated sugar

PIE SHELL
1. Preheat the oven to 350°F.
2. In a food processor, pulse the graham crackers to fine crumbs. Melt the butter and mix it into the graham cracker crumbs. Press the mixture into a springform pan. Bake the pie shell on the middle rack of the oven for 12 minutes. Remove the pie shell from the oven and cool it completely.

CHOCOLATE FILLING
1. Chop both types of chocolate separately, putting the milk chocolate in one bowl and the dark chocolate in another. Heat the whipping cream until it is steaming hot but not boiling. Pour half of the cream over the dark chocolate and the rest over the milk chocolate. Let the mixtures stand for 1 minute, and then stir them until the chocolate is completely melted.
2. Pour the dark chocolate ganache into the pie shell and refrigerate the pie for about 20 minutes, or until the layer has set. Now pour in the milk chocolate ganache. Refrigerate the pie until the filling is set, another 20 minutes or so.

MERINGUE TOPPING
1. Pour the egg whites and sugar into a heatproof bowl and place the bowl over a simmering water bath. Beat the mixture with a hand whisk until it reaches 150°F or the sugar melts (carefully rub a little of the mixture between your fingers to determine whether it is smooth or still granular) and the mixture is hot.
2. Remove the bowl from the water bath and use an electric mixer to beat the meringue until it is quite thick and has cooled. Spread the meringue over the chocolate filling with a spatula and caramelize it with a brûlée torch.

BANOFFEE PIE WITH HONEYCOMB

This banoffee pie is a wonderful classic and one of the easiest pies you can make. I make my banoffee pies in small pans with a little honeycomb on top for extra chew resistance. Honeycomb is a crisp and sweet candy that tastes a little like caramel. If you make it with honey, it will have a distinct honey flavor.

3 small pies, 5¼ inches in diameter, 6–8 servings

PIE SHELL
8 ounces digestive biscuits or graham crackers

7 tablespoons (3½ ounces) butter

HONEYCOMB
¼ cup granulated sugar

1 tablespoon honey or golden syrup

½ teaspoon baking soda

BANANA AND DULCE DE LECHE FILLING
1 can dulce de leche (14 ounces)

3 bananas

1 cup whipping cream

1 ounce dark chocolate (70% cocoa)

TIP: Dip pieces of the honeycomb in melted dark chocolate and let the chocolate set. Amazingly good! If you have any leftover honeycomb, you can save it in an airtight jar. Use it as soon as possible, before it becomes sticky.

PIE SHELL
1. Preheat the oven to 350°F.
2. In a food processor, pulse the digestive biscuits to fine crumbs. Melt the butter and mix it into the cookie crumbs. Divide the mixture among three pie pans and press it into each pan to form the shell. Bake the pie shell on the middle rack of the oven for 12 minutes. Remove the pie shell from the oven and let it cool completely.

HONEYCOMB
1. Line a baking sheet with parchment paper.
2. Pour the sugar into a saucepan and heat it on medium. When the sugar begins to melt around the edge, use a spoon to carefully stir it to the center of the pan until all the sugar has melted and is golden brown.
3. Add the honey and let it melt into the sugar. Remove the pan from the heat and quickly stir in the baking soda. The mixture will immediately begin to bubble up, so you have to work quickly before it hardens. Pour the mixture onto the parchment paper and let it set completely; it will take 20 to 30 minutes.
4. Break the honeycomb into smaller pieces.

BANANA AND DULCE DE LECHE FILLING
1. Spread the dulce de leche in the pie shells. Slice the bananas and arrange them on top. Beat the whipping cream until fluffy and then spoon some onto each pie.
2. Chop the chocolate and sprinkle it over the pies together with the honeycomb bits.

PECAN PIE WITH PHYLLO DOUGH

I was inspired by baklava when I made this pie. Layer on layer of crisp phyllo dough, butter, sugar, nuts, and cinnamon topped by a sweet, creamy filling with nuggets of toasted pecans. The pie puffs up quite a bit while baking, so make sure the pan you choose is at least 2⅛ inches deep.

1 pie, about 8 inches in diameter, 8–10 servings

TOASTED PECANS

7 ounces pecans

FILLING

5¼ tablespoons (2⅔ ounces) butter

6 tablespoons light Muscovado sugar (firmly packed in measuring spoon)

⅓ cup granulated sugar

3 large eggs

6 tablespoons maple syrup or golden syrup

¼ teaspoon sea salt

PIE SHELL

6 sheets frozen phyllo dough (about 9¾ ounces)

5¼ tablespoons (2⅔ ounces) butter

½ ounce toasted pecans (from nuts above)

¼ cup granulated sugar

½ teaspoon ground cinnamon

TIP: Buy nuts in bulk. It is often cheaper than individual bags of nuts, and you can buy exactly the amount you need.

TOASTED PECANS

1. Preheat the oven to 300°F.
2. Place the pecans on a baking sheet lined with parchment paper and toast them on the middle rack of the oven for 12 to 14 minutes, until they take on a little color and smell nutty. Check them often at the end of toasting time, as they can burn easily.
3. Remove the pecans from the oven and let them cool. Break the nuts into large pieces.

FILLING

1. Melt the butter.
2. Whisk the Muscovado sugar, granulated sugar, and eggs in a bowl. Add the syrup and salt and the melted butter. Set the mixture aside.

ASSEMBLING AND BAKING THE PIE

1. Thaw the phyllo dough following the instructions on the package.
2. Melt the butter for the pie shell and brush a pie pan with a little of it. Drizzle brush the melted butter on the top of the first sheet of phyllo dough and lay it in the pan. Drape the dough over the edge and make sure the overhang is 2 to 2½ inches around.
3. Finely chop about ½ ounce of the toasted pecans and mix them with the granulated sugar and cinnamon in a small bowl. Sprinkle a little of the sugar and nut mixture over the first layer of phyllo dough.
4. Brush the second sheet of phyllo dough with butter and lay it in the pan (overlap the layers so that the whole edge all around is covered with phyllo). Sprinkle on some of the sugar and nut mixture. Brush a new sheet of phyllo dough with butter and continue layering the dough with the sugar/nut mix in the pan. Finish with a sheet of phyllo with butter drizzled over it.
5. Mix the remainder of the nuts into the prepared filling and pour the filling into the pie pan. Fold up the edges of the phyllo dough over the pie and press them to stay in place.
6. Raise the oven temperature to 350°F. Bake the pie on the lower rack of the oven for 45 to 50 minutes or until the filling has set. Remove the pie from the oven and let it cool for at least 1 hour before cutting. Serve with whipped cream or Vanilla Ice Cream (page 137), if desired.

CHOCOLATE PIE

This chocolate pie is unbelievably good and reminds me a little of mud cake. The dough is tasty with stout, a dark, flavorful beer that goes particularly well with chocolate. The rye flour in the dough gives it a nutty character, but all-purpose flour can be used instead.

1 pie, about 8 inches in diameter, 8–10 servings

PIECRUST

6 tablespoons rye flour

¾ cup all-purpose flour

1 tablespoon granulated sugar

¼ teaspoon sea salt

12 tablespoons (5¼ ounces) cold butter

3–4 tablespoons cold stout or ice-cold water

CHOCOLATE FILLING

4 tablespoons (1¾ ounces) butter

2 eggs

1¼ cups granulated sugar

4 tablespoons cocoa

2 tablespoons all-purpose flour

¼ teaspoon sea salt

⅔ cup evaporated milk (store bought or homemade, following the recipe below)

PIECRUST

1. Mix the rye and all-purpose flours, the sugar, and the salt in a bowl. Dice the butter and add it to the flour mixture. Use your fingers to pinch in the butter until the dough is crumbly.
2. Add the stout (begin with the smaller amount and gradually add more if the mixture is dry) and mix it in with a fork. If you pick up a bit of the dough and it coheres when pressed together, it has enough liquid. If it seems a little dry, add more liquid.
3. Lay a piece of plastic wrap over the dough, flatten the dough somewhat, and then cover the dough completely with plastic wrap. Refrigerate the dough for at least 1 hour, preferably overnight.

ASSEMBLING AND BAKING THE PIE

1. On a floured work surface, roll out the dough until it is ⅛ inch thick. Lay the dough in the pie pan and trim the edge, leaving a small overhang. Use the rest of the dough to make some small braids, if desired. Brush the edge of the pie with a little water. Gently press the braids around the edge. Freeze the pie while you prepare the filling.
2. Preheat the oven to 350°F.
3. To make the filling, melt the butter in a saucepan, then remove from heat.
4. In a large bowl, whisk the egg and sugar together until fluffy, about 1 minute.
5. In another bowl, mix the cocoa, flour, and salt, and then stir a little of the mixture into the evaporated milk. Add the cocoa/milk mixture to the egg mixture and then stir in the rest of the evaporated milk as well as the melted butter. Stir until smooth.
6. Remove the pie shell from the freezer and pour in the filling. Bake the pie on the lower rack of the oven for 50 to 55 minutes, until the filling is almost set but still a little wobbly in the center. Remove the pie from the oven and let it cool at least 1 hour before serving. Vanilla Ice Cream (page 137) or lightly whipped cream will be quite good with the pie, if desired.

HOMEMADE EVAPORATED MILK

Get out a small, heavy-bottom saucepan. Pour in ⅔ cup of water and stand a one-use wooden skewer upright in the water. Mark the water level on the skewer by cutting a mark on it.

Pour out the water and pour in 1¾ cups whole milk. Heat the milk until it begins to steam and then continue heating it on low heat. Stir constantly with a wooden spoon or a heatproof spatula so that the milk doesn't burn on the bottom. When the level of the milk goes down to the mark on the skewer, the milk is ready, about 30 minutes. Let the milk cool.

PIE WITH PEANUT BUTTER AND CHOCOLATE

This peanut butter and chocolate pie is groovy—sweet, a little salty, a little tart, and unbelievably creamy. It's perfect for those who love the combination of peanut butter and chocolate. I sent a few servings home to my little brother, who, according to my mother, yelled from his room that it was the best pie he had ever eaten. The pie should be served refrigerator cold so it won't get too soft.

1 pie, about 8 inches in diameter, 8–10 servings

PIE SHELL

7 ounces Ballerina cookies (Swedish chocolate–hazelnut cream filled) or Oreos

2⅔ ounces salted peanuts

2 tablespoons (1 ounce) butter

PEANUT BUTTER FILLING

7 ounces cream cheese, at room temperature

⅔ cup confectioners' sugar

¾ cup peanut butter, at room temperature (without sugar or salt)

3½ ounces milk chocolate

¾ cup whipping cream

GANACHE

1¾ ounces milk chocolate

1¾ ounces dark chocolate (70% cacao)

6 tablespoons whipping cream

TOPPING

1¾ ounces milk chocolate

1¾ ounces salted peanuts

PIE SHELL

1. Preheat the oven to 350°F.
2. In a food processor, pulse the cookies and peanuts to fine crumbs.
3. Melt the butter and mix it with the crumbs; press the mixture into a springform pan.
4. Bake the pie shell on the middle rack of the oven for 10 minutes. Remove the pie shell from the oven and let it cool.

PEANUT BUTTER FILLING

1. In a bowl, beat the cream cheese and confectioners' sugar until creamy. Beat in the peanut butter.
2. Melt the milk chocolate over a hot-water bath and let it cool to lukewarm.
3. Whisk the melted chocolate into the peanut butter cream.
4. Beat the whipping cream until it is fluffy but not too firm and then fold it into the peanut butter and chocolate mixture. Pour the filling into the pie shell, smoothing the surface with a spatula. Refrigerate the pie for at least 2 hours, preferably overnight.

GANACHE

1. Chop all the chocolate and put it in a bowl.
2. Heat the whipping cream in a small saucepan until it is quite hot but not boiling. Pour the warm cream over the chocolate, let it stand for 30 seconds, and then stir the ganache until it is smooth. Let the ganache cool at room temperature until it has thickened slightly and then spread it over the pie.
3. To make the topping, sliver the milk chocolate and chop the peanuts; sprinkle them over the pie.

PUMPKIN PIE WITH CHOCOLATE

For an extragood and crisp surface on your pumpkin pie, try sprinkling a couple of tablespoons of raw or granulated sugar in a thin layer over the pie and then caramelize it with a brûlée torch immediately before serving.

The pumpkin puree can be made a day ahead; in that case, pour it into a jar and store it in the refrigerator.

1 pie, about 8 inches in diameter, 8–10 servings

PUMPKIN PUREE

1 small sugar pumpkin or butternut squash, about 2½ pounds

PIECRUST

1¼ cups all-purpose flour

1 tablespoon granulated sugar

¼ teaspoon sea salt

¼ teaspoon ground cardamom

1 egg yolk (reserve the egg white for the glaze)

9 tablespoons (4½ ounces) cold butter

3–5 tablespoons ice-cold water

PUMPKIN FILLING

1 pound pumpkin puree (see above)

6 tablespoons granulated sugar

⅓ cup light Muscovado sugar (firmly packed in measuring cup)

2 large eggs

1 teaspoon ground cinnamon

¼ teaspoon ground ginger

¼ teaspoon ground clove

½ teaspoon sea salt

1 cup whipping cream

3 tablespoons cocoa

PUMPKIN PUREE

1. Preheat the oven to 350°F.
2. Cut the pumpkin down the center lengthwise. Scoop out the seeds (save and toast them), and place the halves, cut side down, on a baking sheet lined with parchment paper. Roast the pumpkin on the middle rack of the oven for about 50 minutes, until soft.
3. Remove the pumpkin from the oven and let it cool. Scoop out the pumpkin and pulse it to a fine puree in a processor.

PIECRUST

1. Mix the flour, granulated sugar, salt, and cardamom in a bowl. Whisk the egg yolk and add it to the mixture. Add the butter. Use your fingers to pinch in the butter until the dough is crumbly.
2. Add the cold water gradually and mix it in with a fork. If the dough coheres when pressed together, it has enough liquid.
3. Lay a piece of plastic wrap over the dough, flatten the dough somewhat, and then cover the dough completely with plastic wrap. Refrigerate the dough for at least 1 hour, preferably overnight.

ASSEMBLING AND BAKING THE PIE

1. On a floured work surface, roll out the dough until it is ⅛ inch thick. Lay the rolled-out dough in a pie pan and pinch the edge into a crimped border (see page 18). Refrigerate the crust while you prepare the filling. Save any remaining dough in the refrigerator to use later to make some small leaves.
2. Preheat the oven to 435°F.
3. To make the filling, beat the pumpkin puree, granulated sugar, Muscovado sugar, eggs, cinnamon, ginger, clove, and salt together in a large bowl. Stir in the whipping cream.
4. Pour the cocoa into another bowl and then mix about one-third of the pumpkin filling into it, stirring until it is smooth.
5. Remove the pie shell from the refrigerator and brush it entirely with egg white.
6. Layer the chocolate/pumpkin mixture and the pumpkin-only filling in the pie shell. Repeat for several layers. Use a skewer to swirl the layers together. Bake the pie on the lower rack of the oven for 10 minutes; reduce the temperature to 350°F and bake for another 50 to 60 minutes, until the pie is relatively firm but still a little wobbly in the center. Remove from the oven and let cool completely. Leave the oven on.
7. Roll out the rest of the dough until about ⅛ inch thin. Cut out leaves with a knife; place them on parchment paper and freeze for 5 minutes. Lay the parchment paper on a baking sheet and bake on the middle rack of the oven for 10 to 12 minutes.
8. Garnish the pie with leaves and serve with Maple Syrup Whipped Cream (page 141).

| PIE TOPPINGS |

VANILLA ICE CREAM
About 2½ cups ice cream

This ice cream is so smooth and good that it perfectly complements every kind of berry and fruit pie.

1 vanilla bean
¾ cup whole milk
6 tablespoons granulated sugar
¼ teaspoon sea salt
3 large egg yolks
1¼ cups whipping cream

1. Split the vanilla bean lengthwise and scrape out the seeds. Combine the milk, sugar, salt, vanilla seeds, and the bean pod in a saucepan. Stir as you heat the mixture to the boiling point. Remove the pan from the heat and put a lid on it. Let the mixture steep for 30 minutes.
2. Lightly whisk the egg yolks in a bowl.
3. Reheat the milk mixture and then, stirring constantly, slowly pour the hot milk over the egg yolks. Pour the entire mixture back into the saucepan and heat it as you whisk it until it thickens, so that it coats the back of a spoon. (**NOTE**: Do not let the mixture boil.)
4. Pour the whipping cream into a bowl and place a sieve over the bowl. Pour the warm milk/egg mixture through the sieve and blend it into the whipping cream.
5. Let the mixture cool. Cover the bowl with plastic wrap and refrigerate it until the mixture is completely cold, preferably overnight.
6. Process the mixture in an ice cream machine until the ice cream is ready and then pour it into a bowl. Freeze the ice cream for 2 to 3 hours before serving.

CARAMEL ICE CREAM
About ½ quart ice cream

A wonderful creamy ice cream with a caramel flavor. It goes perfectly with, for example, Classic Apple Pie (page 30).

1 cup whole milk
⅔ cup whipping cream
½ teaspoon vanilla extract
⅔ cup granulated sugar
3½ tablespoons (1¾ ounces) butter
¼ teaspoon sea salt
3 large egg yolks
1–2 teaspoons dark rum (optional)

1. Pour ½ cup of the milk in a bowl and place a sieve over the bowl. Pour the remaining ½ cup of milk into a saucepan; add the whipping cream and vanilla extract. Heat the mixture over low heat.
2. Pour ½ cup of the sugar into another saucepan and heat it on medium. When the sugar begins to melt around the edges, use a spoon to carefully stir the sugar to the center of the pan until all the sugar has melted and is golden brown. Add the butter to the melted sugar, a small amount at a time, stirring between each addition.
3. Very carefully, pour the warm milk/cream mixture into the sugar/butter mixture—be careful, as it can bubble very suddenly. Carefully stir this mixture until it is well blended, and then remove the pan with this caramel cream from the heat. Add the salt.
4. Whisk the egg yolks with the reserved 1½ tablespoons of sugar in a small bowl. Stir in a little of the warm caramel cream. Pour this mixture back into the saucepan and heat it as you whisk until it thickens. (**NOTE**: Do not let the mixture boil.) Pour the mixture through the sieve into the reserved milk and then blend it in. Add the rum, if desired. Let the mixture cool, over a cold-water bath, if desired. Cover the bowl with plastic wrap and refrigerate it until the mixture is completely cold, preferably overnight.
5. Process the mixture in an ice cream machine until the ice cream is ready, and then pour it into a bowl. Freeze for 2 to 3 hours before serving.

CRÈME FRAÎCHE ICE CREAM WITH HONEY
About ½ quart ice cream

This ice cream is creamy and fresh, using crème fraîche instead of whipping cream.

6 tablespoons water
⅓ cup granulated sugar
Finely grated zest of ¼ lemon
1 tablespoon honey
Pinch of sea salt
¼ cup whole milk
¾ cup crème fraîche

1. Heat the water, sugar, and lemon zest in a saucepan until the sugar dissolves. Remove the pan from the heat, stir in the honey and salt, and let the contents cool completely, preferably over a cold-water bath.
2. Add the milk and crème fraîche to the saucepan and

stir it with a hand whisk until the mixture is smooth. Cover the saucepan with a lid and refrigerate it until the mixture is completely cold.

3. Process the mixture in an ice-cream machine until the ice cream is ready and then pour it into a bowl. Freeze the ice cream for 2 to 3 hours before serving.

VANILLA SAUCE
About 3 cups sauce

What's an apple pie without vanilla sauce?

1¼ cups whole milk
1¼ cups whipping cream
1 vanilla bean
6 large egg yolks
⅓ cup granulated sugar

1. Mix the milk and cream in a saucepan. Split the vanilla bean lengthwise, scrape out the seeds, and add the seeds and the bean pod to the milk mixture. Heat this mixture on low until it is steaming hot. Stir occasionally.
2. Place a sieve over a bowl.
3. Whisk the egg yolks and sugar in a small bowl until the sugar crystals have dissolved and the mixture has lightened somewhat.
4. Pour about half of the hot milk mixture over the egg yolks, stirring to blend. Pour this mixture back into the saucepan with the remaining milk mixture and heat it over medium heat. Stirring constantly with a hand whisk, heat the mixture until it has thickened slightly. (**NOTE**: Do not let the mixture boil.)
5. Strain the sauce into the prepared bowl. Place the bowl over a cold-water bath to speed up the cooling process.

CARAMEL VANILLA SAUCE
About 3 cups sauce

This caramel vanilla sauce approximates a blend of caramel sauce and vanilla sauce is completely fantastic and may remind you a little of the taste of crème brûlée.

1¼ cups whole milk
1¼ cups whipping cream
½ teaspoon sea salt
1 vanilla bean

6 large egg yolks
⅔ cup granulated sugar

1. Mix the milk, cream, and salt in a saucepan. Split the vanilla bean lengthwise, scrape out the seeds, and add the seeds and the bean pod to the milk mixture. Heat the mixture on low heat until it is steaming hot. Stir occasionally. Remove the saucepan from the heat and put a lid on the pan.
2. Place a sieve over a bowl.
3. Whisk the egg yolks and 1½ tablespoons of the sugar in a small bowl until the sugar has dissolved.
4. Pour the remaining ½ cup of sugar into another saucepan and heat it over medium. When the sugar begins to melt around the edges, use a spoon to carefully stir the sugar to the center of the pan until all the sugar has melted and is golden brown. Reduce the heat and pour in the warm milk mixture very carefully—beware, as it can bubble up suddenly. Carefully stir the mixture until it is well blended.
5. Pour about half of the warm caramel mixture over the egg yolk mixture, stirring to blend. Pour this mixture back into the saucepan and heat on medium. Stirring constantly with a hand whisk, heat the mixture until it has slightly thickened.
6. Immediately strain the sauce into the prepared bowl. Place the bowl over a cold-water bath to speed up the cooling process.

[Flavor Variations]
Vanilla Sauce with Orange

2 tablespoons Cointreau or freshly squeezed orange juice
1 teaspoon finely grated orange zest
1 batch Vanilla Sauce or Caramel Vanilla Sauce (cold)

Stir the Cointreau and orange zest into the cold sauce.

Spiced Vanilla Sauce with Cognac

1–2 tablespoons cognac
1 batch Vanilla Sauce or Caramel Vanilla Sauce (cold)
½ teaspoon ground cinnamon
½ teaspoon ground cardamom

Stir the cognac into the sauce, beginning with the smaller amount and increasing it if you want a more pronounced cognac flavor. In a small bowl, blend the cinnamon and cardamom with a tablespoon of the sauce mixture and then blend it into the remaining sauce.

VANILLA CREAM
About 2 ¼ cups

Vanilla cream is a fluffier version of vanilla sauce. I use the same type of recipe as for vanilla sauce, although I add whipped cream at the end.

⅔ cup whole milk
½ vanilla bean
3 large egg yolks
3 tablespoons granulated sugar
⅔ cup whipping cream

1. Pour the milk into a saucepan. Split the vanilla bean lengthwise, scrape out the seeds, and add the seeds and the bean pod to the milk. Heat the mixture on low until it is steaming hot. Stir occasionally. Remove the pan from the heat and put a lid on it.
2. Place a sieve over a bowl.
3. Whisk the egg yolks and sugar in a small bowl until the sugar crystals have dissolved and the mixture lightens a little.
4. Pour about half of the hot milk mixture over the egg yolks, stirring to blend. Pour the mixture back into the saucepan, stirring to blend, and heat on medium. Stirring constantly with a hand whisk, heat the mixture until it has slightly thickened. (**NOTE**: Do not let it boil.)
5. Strain the sauce into the prepared bowl. Place the bowl over a cold-water bath to speed up the cooling process.
6. Whip the cream until it is quite thick and then stir it into the vanilla sauce.

CARAMEL SAUCE WITH RUM
About ¾ cup

This fantastically good caramel sauce is excellent for drizzling over Banana Cream Pie (page 114) or for serving with Classic Apple Pie (page 30).

6 tablespoons granulated sugar
3½ tablespoons (1¾ ounces) cold butter
¼ cup whipping cream
¼ teaspoon sea salt
1 tablespoon dark rum (optional)

1. Pour the sugar into a heavy-bottom saucepan and heat it on medium. When the sugar begins to melt around the edges, use a spoon to carefully stir the sugar to the center of the pan until all the sugar has melted and is golden brown.
2. Dice the butter and add it to the melted sugar, one bit at a time, stirring constantly. Add the cream very carefully, as the mixture may bubble up. Stir until the caramel is smooth and then add the salt and, if desired, the rum. Pour the caramel sauce into a heat-proof jar and let it cool to room temperature.

MAPLE CREAM
About ¾ cup

This creamy spread is simply pure maple syrup that is boiled, cooled, and then sti red to a thick, wonderful, spread-able cream not unlike butter in consistency. This takes time and strong arms but is absolutely perfect when you want a concentrated maple syrup flavor.

¾ cup + 1 tablespoon genuine maple syrup (grade A)
¼ teaspoon sea salt

1. Prepare a cold-water bath in a large bowl, or fill a dishpan with a few inches of cold water.
2. Pour the maple syrup and salt into a heavy-bottom saucepan with high sides and bring the syrup to a boil without stirring. The temperature should come to 230°F to 234°F as measured on a candy thermometer. Immediately transfer the pan to the cold-water bath and let it cool to body temperature (leave the thermometer in the saucepan).
3. Remove the pan from the water bath and stir the syrup with a wooden spoon until it becomes very light and creamy and looks about like peanut butter. This can take up to 30 minutes if you stir by hand. It is also fine to beat the mixture with an electric beater, but let the mixer rest every couple of minutes so the motor doesn't overheat. Pour the cream into a clean jar and store it in the refrigerator. If the cream gets too hard in the refrigerator, bring it to room temperature before using, or heat it up for a few seconds in the microwave.

MAPLE SYRUP WHIPPED CREAM
About 4 servings

Perfect for Pumpkin Pie with Chocolate (page 133).

¾ cup whipping cream
2 tablespoons Maple Cream (see previous recipe)

Whip the cream until it is slightly thick. Add the maple syrup butter and beat the cream until it is firm.

WHIPPED HONEY CRÈME FRAÎCHE
About 1 cup

This whipped topping is sweet but also a little sour, which would be perfect served with Galette with Strawberries and Rhubarb (page 71) or Rhubarb Slab Pie (page 47).

6 tablespoons whipping cream
6 tablespoons crème fraîche
2 tablespoons honey
½ teaspoon vanilla extract

Blend all the ingredients in a bowl and beat to the desired consistency, to soft peaks.

HOMEMADE MASCARPONE
About 1¼ cups mascarpone cheese

Mascarpone is an Italian fresh cheese that I love to use for baked goods. The best part is that it isn't particularly difficult to make, and it requires only two ingredients. Make sure to use cream without any additives.

2¼ cups whipping cream
1 tablespoon freshly squeezed lemon juice

1. Pour the whipping cream into a heavy-bottom saucepan. Carefully heat the cream on low. The cream should reach 185°F. Stir occasionally and make sure the cream doesn't burn on the bottom. This should take 20 to 30 minutes.
2. When the cream reaches 185°F, stir in the lemon juice. Continue holding the temperature to 185°F, carefully stirring for 5 to 6 minutes. The cream should thicken noticeably but continue to be runny.
3. Remove the pan from the heat and prepare a cold-water bath in a pan or bowl. Place the pan in the water bath and let it remain until the mixture is completely cold. During this step, the mixture will continue to thicken.
4. Line a sieve with 2 to 3 layers of coffee filters and place the sieve over a bowl. Pour the mixture through the coffee filters. Lay a plate over the sieve to cover the mixture and bowl and refrigerate it for 8 hours.
5. After 8 hours, the mascarpone should be thick and creamy. Turn the mascarpone out onto a plate and remove the coffee filters. You can discard the small amount of liquid that has drained into the bowl underneath. Store the cheese in an airtight jar in the refrigerator. It will keep for about 1 week in the refrigerator.

HOMEMADE CRÈME FRAÎCHE
About 1¼ cups

It is important for this crème fraîche recipe that you use cream without any additives. Homemade crème fraîche needs to be made in a rather warm place. If, like me, you have a cool house, it's a good idea to turn the oven on to a very low heat so that it becomes somewhat warmer than room temperature; turn the oven off and then let the jar stand inside the oven or leave the jar standing on the stovetop after the oven has been on.

If you don't use all the buttermilk or sour milk at once, you can freeze it in an ice cube tray and then thaw it when you want to make crème fraîche. This is perfect for when you have cream in the refrigerator that you don't quite know what to do with.

1 cup heavy whipping cream
4 tablespoons buttermilk or natural sour milk

1. Mix the whipping cream and buttermilk in a jar and put the lid on top. Let the mixture stand at room temperature in a warm place for 12 to 15 hours. The mixture should have thickened a little.
2. Stir the mixture and refrigerate it for 6 to 8 hours. After 6 hours, the mixture might still be loose, but stir it with a spoon and you'll have a thick and creamy crème fraîche.

Index

Acknowledgments and Credits

THANK YOU!
Christian, my best friend in the whole
world, because you tasted everything
with pleasure and helped with
everything.

My great family and friends who come
and pick up the taste samples. You are
the best!

Editor Eva and publisher Martin for your
enthusiasm, your knowledge, and most
of all, your patience.

Katy, for the lovely design.

Kalklitir, because you drove the backgrounds painted with your wonderful
colors right to my door when I didn't
have enough backgrounds.

All the fantastic blog readers; without you
none of this would have been possible.

Roost Books
An imprint of Shambhala Publications, Inc.
4720 Walnut Street
Boulder, Colorado 80301
roostbooks.com

© 2016 by Linda Lomelino
English translation © 2017 by Shambhala Publications, Inc.
Photography: Linda Lomelino
Graphic styling: Katy Kimbell
Translation into English: Carol Huebscher Rhoades

First published by Bonnier Fakta, Stockholm, Sweden.
Published in the English language by arrangement with Bonnier Rights, Stockholm. Sweden.
www.bonnierfakta.se

First U.S. Edition
Printed in China

♾ This edition is printed on acid-free paper that meets the
American National Standards Institute Z39.48 Standard.
♻ Shambhala Publications makes every effort to print on recycled paper.
For more information please visit www.shambhala.com.

Distributed in the United States by Penguin Random House LLC and in Canada by
Random House of Canada Ltd

Designed by Katy Kimbell

Library of Congress Cataloging-in-Publication Data

Names: Lomelino, Linda, author. | Translation of: Lomelino, Linda. Lomelinos pajer.
Title: Lomelino's pies: a sweet celebration of pies, galettes, and tarts / Linda Lomelino.
Other titles: Lomelinos pajer. English
Description: Boulder: Roost, 2017. | "First published by Bonnier Fakta, Stockholm, Sweden." |
Includes bibliographical references and index.
Identifiers: LCCN 2016030933 | ISBN 9781611804560 (hardcover: alk. paper)
Subjects: LCSH: Pies. | LCGFT: Cookbooks.
Classification: LCC TX773 .L58423 2017 | DDC 641. 86/52—dc23 LC record available at
https://lccn.loc.gov/2016030933